Chasing Rainbows

A book for individuals who reside in "Barren Land" -
A place where seeds don't fully grow and flowers don't fully bloom.

Sharhonda L. Ford

Chasing Rainbows

Copyright © 2020 by Sharhonda L. Ford

ISBN 978-1-954450-00-4

All rights reserved. Published by She HOPES Media Publishing, LLC.

No part of this book may be reproduced or transmitted in any form or by any means without written permission of the author.

This book is designed to provide inspiration and motivation to our readers. The author is not providing psychological, legal, or any other kind of professional advice and is the sole expression of the author. No warranties or guarantees are expressed or implied.

Scripture quotations marked (ESV) are taken from The ESV® Bible (The Holy Bible, English Standard Version®), copyright © 2001 by Crossway, a publishing ministry of Good News Publishers. Used by permission. All rights reserved.

Scripture quotations marked (NIV) are taken from the Holy Bible, New International Version®, NIV®. Copyright © 1973, 1978, 1984, 2011 by Biblica, Inc.™ Used by permission of Zondervan. All rights reserved worldwide. www.zondervan.com The "NIV" and "New International Version" are trademarks registered in the United States Patent and Trademark Office by Biblica, Inc.™

Scripture quotations marked (NKJV) are taken from the New King James Version®. Copyright © 1982 by Thomas Nelson. Used by permission. All rights reserved.

Scripture quotations marked (AMP) are taken from the Amplified Bible, Copyright © 1954, 1958, 1962, 1964, 1965, 1987 by The Lockman Foundation. Used by permission.

The KJV is public domain in the United States.

Cover credit:
J.L. Woodson for Woodson Creative Studio

Editing credit:
Yakisha Bookard

This book is dedicated to my husband, best friend, and life partner, Kirey, who has carried me, covered me and prayed for me as I journeyed through Barren Land. May Jesus always give him what he needs on and for this journey. I love you and I thank God that He chose us for one another.

Tribute to my Mommy, Patricia A. Moseley.

You call me your star, but you are mine.

Thank you for showing me what love looks like. Your unconditional love, devotion, and commitment to our family gives me strength. You taught me things I long to teach my children. The bond we have as mother and daughter is unparalleled. I will cherish our relationship forever.

Love you, Mommy

In memory of the seeds that never fully bloomed.

According to Parents.com, a rainbow baby is "a baby born subsequent to a miscarriage, stillbirth, or the death of an infant from natural causes".

Chasing Rainbows was written as a Devotional Guide for couples who may be journeying through the sorrows of their own "Barren Land". This book was intended primarily to uplift women; however, since "Barren Land" is a journey wives and husbands often take together, feel free to invite your spouse to join you in finding triumph in tragedy.

Acknowledgments

To my amazing Lord and Savior, Jesus Christ, thank you for keeping me when I felt like giving up. Your promise, purpose and plan for my life are far greater than anything I can imagine. Thank you for reminding me that being made in your image is enough and I have value regardless.

To my amazing nieces (Sharee, Mariah and Zoe), nephews (Zion and Christian) and Godchildren (Cailyn, Khloe and Israel), thank you for allowing me to love you as if you were my own. To my Dunia, thank you for being the one to call me "Ma" and for allowing me to play that role in your life when God saw fit. You will always be "Mama's" baby!

Introduction

One Friday evening, as I headed back to my house from an evening of fellowship and prayer, my sister-in-Christ suggested we ride together. This gave us time to catch up and share what God was doing in our lives as we were coming and going. Earlier that night, I had become overwhelmed with grief during our time of fellowship and prayer and I couldn't figure out what was happening. My heart was breaking. This time, the heartbreak felt different. The difference was, I was grieving brokenness, but not my own. I was accustomed to crying and grieving around women and mothers. There were (and, at times, still are) seasons where seeing women pregnant or who have children would bring me unbearable sorrow. In the past, those experiences were a constant reminder of the very thing I desired but did not have. I longed to carry a child full-term. I longed to get to the point where I could feel more than the "weirdness" of a first trimester pregnancy. I longed to experience the miracle of childbirth. Pregnant women and mothers reminded me of the shame I felt on this journey I call "Barren Land".

But this grief was different. This feeling was different. This brokenness was different. This brokenness was not about me. As a Licensed Clinical Mental Health Counselor, I work with women and couples on a regular basis. Seeing the brokenness in marriages is heartbreaking. Knowing the grief of longing for something to be whole that is continually broken is what caused my sorrow that evening. I grieved broken marriages and women who had no one to talk to. I equated the feeling of sorrow and grief for women in broken marriages to the level of grief I felt in the desire to be free from Barren Land.

Although I was grieving, this time, I was not actually hurting. After many days and years of suffering and grieving for myself, this was the first time that I realized I was experiencing God's peace in *my* situation. I finally had peace that the rainbow may never come. What an incredible feeling! I spent thirteen years in bondage to the grief, sorrow, shame, uncertainty, resentment, bitterness, embarrassment, silence, anger and struggle of infertility (trouble conceiving or delays in conceiving). And just like that, without notice, without thought, I realized that when I focused on the thought of not having a baby, when I imagined what life would be like if God NEVER allowed me to carry a child full-term - I HAD PEACE! What a sense of Freedom! This was a feeling I longed for and never imagined I would experience; and this night, God showed me His peace. Thank you, Jesus!

******

Have you ever wanted something so badly that the absence of that thing becomes ALL you can think about? Have you ever thought that without it, life would have no value, no meaning? Maybe you thought that because you didn't have it something was wrong with you. What would *other* people say or think about you? What do *you* think about you? Are you less than because of this absence?

There are so many questions just like those that have come to my mind over the last 13 years. Many of them I have held in secret. Sometimes, I shared them with a heart of shame, fear, disgrace, embarrassment and/or resentment. Sometimes, I cradled them as I cried sitting in the bottom of my shower or lying in a fetal position on my bed, on the floor or even in the closet. Sometimes, all I could do was cry. No thoughts. No emotions. No questions. Nothing.

Anger. Fear. Hopelessness. Embarrassment. Doubt. Shame. Jealousy. Envy. Grief. Despair. Loneliness. Hatred. Numb. I felt and experienced emotions I did not know I could feel, and on many days, I had no idea from where they came. I just prayed that I would *never* feel them again. Never. But they kept coming back.

Merriam-Webster defines *barren*[1] as "unproductive and unfruitful". Women who are barren carry a burden that others cannot conceptualize. For women who desire to have children naturally, being "unproductive" can be damaging to them physically, emotionally, mentally, and spiritually. How can women journey through the seasons of infertility and still be physically, emotionally, mentally, and spiritually whole? In this book, I intend to discuss the challenges of infertility and the triumph of trusting God's plan for my life through prayer, God's word, and therapy. It is my prayer that the tools I used in my experience and on my journey will be valuable and encouraging to you either individually or with your spouse.

Each topic introduced in this book represents a stopping point in Barren Land. While I know every couple will not have the same journey; each topic is intended to inspire, encourage and heal the brokenness, heartache, despair, grief and many other powerful emotions caused by infertility, miscarriage, stillbirth, and the "trying to conceive" (TTC) experience.

So, let us journey this "Barren Land" together as I unveil the promising yet painful truth of my challenges, trials, and triumphs. May God unfold His truths about trusting Him when our "fantasy

---

[1] "Barren." The Merriam-Webster.com Dictionary, Merriam-Webster Inc., https://www.merriam-webster.com/dictionary/barren. Accessed 22 January 2020.

doesn't match our reality" (something my daddy used to say to me). Grab some tissues, a great cup of tea or coffee, a pen and prepare to be healed, set free, and delivered from the bondage of shame, guilt, and grief associated with the journey through Barren Land.

Table of Contents

Chapter	Page
What is Happening?	9
Month by Month	14
Why is this Happening?	19
God, I Am Angry	23
The Cycle Woes	27
TTC	31
Miscarriage	36
Honey, I'm So Sorry	42
Oh, No! Not Again!	46
Let's Give it a Try	50
The Diagnosis	56
The Prognosis	60
It's Not Happening…Now What?	65
Look Who's Pregnant Now!	70
Who Can I Talk To?	75
No, Not Tonight	81
I'm Not Woman Enough	87
Fault Doesn't Matter	92
What Do You Say?	97
When is Enough, Enough?	102
Alternatives to Natural Childbirth	107
My Marriage is Hurting	112
You're NOT the Only One Suffering	117
Do You Hear That?	122
Silent Suffering Speaks Volumes	122
Hello, My Name is Shame	127
Everyone is Having a Baby	132
Except Me	132

Why Do They Ask?	137
Choosing to Tell Your Story	142
God Has NOT Failed You	147
Finding Purpose in Pain	152
Triumph from Tragedy	158
Too Soon to Tell	163
Saturated in Shame	167
Forgiveness – Abortion and Infertility	172
A Chat with the Author	177

What is Happening?

You're married now! How exciting to begin this new journey? You met, fell in love, courted, and now you've made a vow. For better or worse, for richer and poorer, in sickness and in health. Wait! Did you ever wonder what that really means? Sickness *and* in health?

You are all giggles now and you both have decided what a perfect time to grow your family. Lots of talk about girls and boys, names, and desires. The excitement mounts and now... "Let's make a baby!" It's been two weeks and you've already stocked up on pregnancy tests because you'll want to test again and again to see that plus sign multiple times. As the days go by, you're already planning the baby's room theme, looking at Pinterest for ideas, and talking to your friends about your plans for motherhood.

That trip to the bathroom, just days before you plan to take the test and you see a sign the test is not needed. "What in the world? Oh, well. Not this month," you respond matter-of-factly and look forward to next month.

After all, this really is just your first month trying or at least NOT *not* trying 😊. No need for concern. Keep enjoying the process and put those tests away for next month.

Oops! There it goes again. There's a sense of dread here, but no thoughts of defeat or concern. But wait, this is ONLY the second month and you've heard many stories of how it can take some time once you are ready. And, of course, you KNOW everyone's story is different. Carry on! Remember you are a newlywed and all this *trying* is exciting!

Well, three time's a charm! This has got to be it. You're checking the pregnancy tests to make sure they haven't expired and are ready this time to get the countdown going. Those fourteen days seem like they will never come. However, when it does come, it's ALWAYS too soon. Just like that, three times won't be a charm THIS time.

What do you do when three times isn't a charm? You pray. When I talk to other women who are trying or have tried to conceive, this story is so common. The shock factor builds. Before you know it, month by month, hope fades.

During my "What is Happening" season, I found myself comforted by my husband's consoling words, "Don't worry. When it's the Lord's will, it will happen." After all, there was no need for concern. We had gone to the doctor before getting married. "Everything is fine. There should absolutely be no problems," the doctor said. He had been keeping a close eye on things the year before the wedding and making sure we were well-prepared and doing the things necessary for a healthy pregnancy and birth. I wasn't alarmed – just anxious and I knew that God would indeed hear my prayers and answer me.

Continuing to ponder what was happening, I returned to the only place that I find answers that are true, God's word. It was important for me to cling to His promises and to trust in Him with my entire heart. Surely, what was unexplainable to me was planned by God.

A Moment to H.O.P.E.

Have you had an experience like this... you know, the shock of wondering "what's happening"? Have you found yourself patiently waiting each month to take the test only to realize you don't need to take one? Have you taken one anyway – JUST IN CASE? If this sounds familiar to you, take a moment to write your thoughts as you reflect on your personal experience.

Reflections

_____

_____

_____

_____

_____

_____

_____

Prayer

Father, I thank you for your plan for marriage and family. Lord, I do not know what is happening or why you chose this for me. Lord, help me to walk in your plan void of fear or anxiety. In Jesus' name. Amen.

God's Word

Trust in the Lord with all thine heart; and lean not unto thine own understanding. In all thy ways acknowledge him, and he shall direct thy paths.
Proverbs 3:5-6 (ESV)

Month by Month

A new month dawns. The excitement for another opportunity to see if THIS is the month that it happens is upon us. TTC (Trying to Conceive) is one of the most challenging and overwhelming stresses on an individual, a marriage, and/or a family. The goals, the dreams, and the hopes all seem to fade as the months go by.

    I can remember a season where we can say that we *did not try*. For years, we didn't try. We just didn't *NOT* try. We didn't do anything to prevent pregnancy. We didn't do anything (besides enjoy one another 😊). Still, it just didn't happen. Month by month we were faced with the decision of waiting, trusting, or seeking. Do we continue to wait and just see what happens? I mean, is it God's plan that we enjoy each other before growing our family? Do we continue to trust God's plan for our lives, or do we seek help?

    As a Christian, seeking help almost seemed like not trusting God. So, we stood firm and waited, knowing that the will of God is what we want for our lives. As difficult as it was to watch God's will each month, we stood resolute trusting Him and His plan.

    I must be honest, month by month trusting Him and His plan grew harder for me as the months passed. There were months and sometimes years that it wasn't an issue. After marriage, we had a lot going on. We both were sick at different times. Both of our jobs were eliminated at the same time. We both received relocation opportunities at the same time. We had two mortgages and were still trying to figure out what God was doing in our lives. We stood still. We waited on God. For me, though, the wait was becoming overwhelming.

I recall our first miscarriage which was in 2008 on Mother's Day, of all days. A few days after, I shared it with my dad who said to me, "Yawl, just hurry up! I want to be here to meet my next grandchild." That added more pressure for me. He had already lived three years longer than the doctors had given him. I wanted my child to know my father. I did not want to miss that opportunity; so, internally, I *was* rushing.

Month by month is different for each woman. Some want a child in a specific season or month or time of year. No matter the difference, the disappointment of not being pregnant, not seeing a positive result or having Human Chorionic Gonadotropin (HCG) levels that are too low, bear the same pain and disappointment.

They say that this just isn't the time. Well, when is? When is the time? With all my questions and concerns as the months passed, I had to turn to what God's word says that a thousand years are like a day for Him (2 Peter 3:8[2]). So, in my finite wisdom, time

---

[2] 2 Peter 3:8 (ESV): But do not overlook this one fact, beloved, that with the Lord one day is as a thousand years, and a thousand years as one day.

was of essence to achieve my goal; but in His infinite wisdom, time was limitless. There is no end or beginning. To trust Him meant to trust His boundless timing and wisdom as well as His perfect will and plan for our lives.

A Moment to H.O.P.E.

As you reflect on "month by month", take a moment to write down your thoughts. Do you feel rushed to conceive and have a child? How have you managed, "month by month"? Take some time to reflect on your experience.

Reflections

_____

_____

_____

_____

_____

_____

_____

_____

_____

Prayer

Father, it gets challenging each time I see a sign that this is not the month. I know your will is what I want, and I understand that in your sovereignty you have a plan and a purpose for me. Lord, I pray you would give me wisdom, strength, and peace to stand firm, month by month. In Christ's name. Amen.

God's Word

But do not overlook this one fact, beloved, that with the Lord one day is as a thousand years, and a thousand years as one day.
2 Peter 3:8 (ESV)

Why is this Happening?

"Lord, I have done EVERYTHING right! I'm following directions. I am living in a manner that is pleasing to you and the continuous *nos* are a slap in my face!" That is how I felt one day. I was tired of praying, pleading and begging God to have mercy on me and allow me to do the very thing that I thought I should do – *according to HIS* word: "Be fruitful and multiply". (Genesis 1:22 ESV)

I asked God to do the thing that He said in His word that we should do, yet NOTHING. I didn't understand. I had finally surrendered my will to the Lord's. I had waited (*this* time). I didn't have premarital sex with my husband. I kept myself pure. I trusted God's plan for my life, and I yielded to God's perfect will for me. I expected God to move in MY favor. (Well, I guess I was expecting God to do it MY way!)

It's easy to become uncomfortable and impatient when people are asking, "What are you waiting on? When are you going to start a family? Have you talked about having children? Do you both want children?" I put it out of my mind. I had decided I would not let the pressures of individuals push me to be weary. I'd already gone to the doctor. He had already assured me that "everything was ok" and I should "absolutely be fine conceiving". He said, "Just have fun." And we did. We enjoyed one another. We ministered to one another. We prayed, and we waited.

Then NOTHING. For a while we thought, "Hey, we aren't in a rush." There were still a few things we wanted to do before we started a family. It wasn't disappointing that we didn't have children yet. The fear that it *may not* happen was my concern. Kirey was comfortable with God's plan and I was anxious that God's plan would not match my desires (I mean, I am just being honest here).

It's easy to get caught up in the stories you tell to convince others. I began to believe them. "Whatever the Lord's will is." "If it's the Lord's plan, it *will* happen." That was the acceptable response, but did I really mean it? Was I ok if the Lord did not bless us with a child? I wasn't sure yet. This was just the beginning. At this point, the only thing I wanted to know was, "WHY IS THIS HAPPENING... TO ME?"

During my frustration, Psalm 39:7[3] from God's word centered me and reminded me that my hope was in the Lord. In this situation, no matter what was happening, my hope was in the Lord Jesus Christ. In Christ Jesus, we all have hope. No matter what is happening around or to us, we can find strength and peace in God's word.

---

[3] Psalm 39:7 (ESV): And now, O Lord, for what do I wait? My hope is in you.

A Moment to H.O.P.E.

Have you asked yourself, "Why is this happening to me?" Take a moment and write down your thoughts in the space below. Be honest with yourself and take inventory on where you are on this journey. Whether this is your current journey or a place you have been in the past, note what you are feeling when you think of it now.

Reflections

_____

_____

_____

_____

_____

_____

_____

Prayer

Father, forgive me for not trusting your plan and for questioning you. Who am I to question your wisdom and your plan and promise for my life? I know you have a plan for us; and I pray that as we wait on you, you will give us everything we need to stand. Lord, I love you. In Jesus' name. Amen.

God's Word

And now, O Lord, for what do I wait? My hope is in you.
Psalm 39:7 (ESV)

God, I Am Angry

Why is it we are afraid to admit our anger with God? Are we ashamed? Are we afraid? He already knows. God can handle our feelings. One thing about dealing with infertility and the journey of "Chasing Rainbows", is that it was easy to be mad with God. Why? Because in that season, we knew that God was able to do that which we desired. BUT God chose not to. He chose to continue with His plan for our lives and not our own.

    As I talk to women who have experienced these emotions, there is one common thread. That thread is the guilt of being angry with God. Should we be angry? Is it ok? Just today, I spoke with a woman who expressed her anger with God. I smiled inside and maybe she could see my smile on the outside, as well. I smiled because I knew that feeling. I knew that emotion and I knew what it was like to hold the pain and guilt of being angry with God.

    The Bible says, "Be ye angry, yet do not sin." (Ephesians 4:26 ESV). The challenge was that I believe I sinned. I would be so angry with God that I would decide that I would not serve, trust or do anything else for the Lord. I knew that God wasn't at all surprised or concerned about me and my silly rebellion. As soon as I would say it or think it, within minutes it seemed that God would have me talking to or praying with or for someone. Though I knew I was acting in my flesh, that is how angry and broken I was about my unmet expectations. God, where were you and why weren't you answering my prayer?

Being angry with God will NOT change the situation or circumstance. In fact, it may delay the peace that comes along with accepting God's plan for your life. I understand this is not something easy to do; but I say this because it is necessary. I forfeited my peace because I was so busy in my flesh. When I chose to yield to God's will and get some acceptance (as my daddy used to say), things were so much better. I felt better. I ONLY wish I had chosen differently sooner.

Man, being angry seems so silly as I reflect on it. I am praying for you as you read this. For you and your spouse if you have encountered being angry with God. I am interceding for those who know this feeling of anger toward God and I ask Him to regulate your emotions, calm your heart and heal you that your thoughts may not hold you hostage and delay you being saturated in the peace of God. I want this for you and through Christ it is available to you. Ask Him. Seek Him. Trust Him.

A Moment of H.O.P.E.

If you can relate to being angry with God and what it feels like to forfeit your peace, I encourage you to take a moment and write down your experience in the space provided. Look at where you are on this journey. If you are angry with God, read aloud or within the prayer that follows.

Reflections

_____

_____

_____

_____

_____

_____

_____

Prayer

Father, I thank you for your love and kindness despite my actions and rebellion. Lord, thank you for fathering me, even when I stepped away from you. Thank you for loving me and forgiving me. Heal my emotions, Lord, and allow me to walk in the power and promise of your word. God, I know my anger forfeits my peace. I yield my will to yours and submit to your plan for my life. Lord, I trust you and I love you. In Jesus' name. Amen.

God's Word

Cease from anger, and forsake wrath; Do not fret—it only causes harm.

Psalm 37:8 (NKJV)

The Cycle Woes

After realizing we weren't getting pregnant, we did what many couples do. We started paying closer attention. We had not tried. We just had NOT *not* tried (as I mentioned before). We had been busy about life and before we knew it, years had passed.

Each month, we knew when we needed to have sex to be pregnant. We had already been checked out. I was ovulating. We simply needed to "wait". Seriously? Wait! That is one of the most difficult things to do in this season and on this journey. Besides, what are we waiting for? Another failed attempt? Another negative test result? Another miscarriage? Another disappointment? What do we do while we wait? And remind me again, what were we waiting for?

Each month there was a cycle. Month after month after month. With each cycle came another few weeks of grief, depression, disappointment, and sorrow. But I shook it off. My husband would encourage me with one of his favorite statements, "Babe, we're just going to trust the Lord." Somehow, his encouragement was able to restore some semblance of hope.

Honestly, I was tired of hearing that. I was tired of hearing, "Trust the Lord" when I felt the Lord wasn't trustworthy in THIS area. Why would I trust the Lord? I said I did. I thought I did. But did I really? Did I really trust the Lord when He was not answering my prayer? Did I really trust the Lord when I was disappointed with each cycle? Did I really trust the Lord when the thing I wanted most could be possible in and through Him, but He didn't allow it? And, in my opinion, He wouldn't! Did I really trust the Lord? Well... Did I?

  The cycle woes continued and the most difficult part about it was, I was learning my body. I knew when I would conceive and when that pregnancy would end in miscarriage. I was used to the feeling. Becoming numb to the separation and all too familiar with the pain. The cycle woes caused me to begin drifting away from God. Let me put that a little differently. I had begun to drift away from God as a result of the cycle woes. I was extremely uncomfortable with God not answering my prayers and I did not know what to do. I did not know how to respond.

  During this time, I leaned into the Psalms and could recall Psalm 13:1, "How long, Lord?" I was comforted in knowing that God was familiar with my prayer and my plea. I was comforted in remembering that God had a plan for my life and although I could not trace His hand, I knew I could trust His plan.

A Moment to H.O.P.E.

Are you familiar with "cycle woes"? Share your thoughts on your personal experience here. Remember, trusting God is a choice. Drifting away from God is a choice. I know that on this journey, I made the wrong choice many times. But you do not have to. You can lean into God's word and remember God is good and faithful. Remember that no matter how long, God has NOT forgotten you.

Reflections

_____

_____

_____

_____

_____

_____

_____

Prayer

Father God, this is challenging. I do not know what to do as I wait on you. I want to trust you, but sometimes, it is difficult. I cry out to you, "How long, Oh Lord?"[4] I beg of you, Lord, to remember me. I reflect on your word that reminds me to "trust in the Lord with all my heart and lean not to my own understanding"[5]. My understanding is wavering as is my faith at times. Lord, I want to trust you. I need my hope restored. Give me the strength to stand and the patience to wait. In Jesus' name. Amen.

God's Word

How long, O LORD? Will You forget me forever? How long will You hide Your face from me?
Psalm 13:1 (ESV)

---

[4] Psalm 13:1
[5] Proverbs 3:5

TTC

Well, if you knew what TTC was without much thought, then chances are, you are more familiar than you'd like to be with this experience. When I first started reading blogs and doing research, TTC was a common acronym in many conversations.

For those of you who do not know, TTC (Trying to Conceive) is one of the most difficult parts of this journey. Who am I kidding? It is ALL very difficult. It is not easy to plan sex... ensuring timing and temperature are accurate. It's like baking. Everything must be calculated and measured accordingly, or else. Or else, the desired outcome is not reached.

Did we do that? Had we done all of the intricate things that are recommended when TTC? Well, not sure that we really did. My husband was so insistent that the Lord would move in His time; so, for years, that is what we stood on – God's promise (or at least my husband did). We stood on believing God would do it according to His timing. Early on, we had not considered that God would NOT do it. We ONLY believed (ok, maybe I DID doubt God quite a few times), that God was working in *His* time. We knew God's time was NOT our time; so, I stood firm on that truth as often as I could. Not because I wanted to, but because my husband, whom I love and ashamedly, at this point, trusted more than God – said we should.

So, what does TTC look like? TTC is different for many people. It can mean anything from tracking Basal body temperatures and observing cervical mucus for optimal ovulation period, clomid cycles to induce ovulation, and Intrauterine Insemination's (IUI) and In Vitro Fertilization (IVF). That is just naming a few things. No matter what method is used, the prayer is the same, "Lord, PLEASE LET IT WORK THIS TIME!"

How do I know all of this? It certainly was *not* from having a supportive group of women to share. In my experience, there was NO ONE talking about TTC. None of my peers, family or friends had mentioned it to me... possibly because many of those around me didn't seem to have a problem conceiving. Everyone was popping up pregnant and without accident or delay. OK. Maybe a few accidents; but we know God doesn't make mistakes. Right?

TTC was a silent process/journey for me. I didn't share it with my family or my friends and, honestly, I couldn't even comprehend what was happening within myself. I went along trying to act like everything was ok. I was not able to focus on the reality that maybe, just maybe, there was a problem. I also could not come to terms with the process of TTC and that I was navigating through it.

TTC truly is one of the most difficult parts of this journey. What should you try? When should you try? What can you afford? What if this doesn't work? Will there be any viable eggs? The list of questions goes on and on. There are more questions related to TTC than chapters in this book and all of them, yes, all of them, may lead to anger, fear, shame, hopelessness, doubt, grief, resentment, and frustration.

I faced powerful emotions during the process of trying to conceive. I was happy and sad, and fearful and mad. I experienced a myriad of emotions; however, clinging to God's word carried me through. Singing songs of praise like "Tis so sweet to trust in Jesus" and praying God's word over my life gave me strength. It gave me hope. It gave me faith. Faith in the promise and plan God had for my life as in Jeremiah 29:11[6].

---

[6] Jeremiah 29:11 (ESV): For I know the plans I have for you, declares the LORD, plans for welfare and not for evil, to give you a future and a hope.

A Moment to H.O.P.E.

Take a moment and share your thoughts about your personal TTC journey, past or present, below. Once you have reflected on your personal journey, pray the prayer that follows.

Reflections

Prayer

Lord, we understand that you are in control. We need to trust your plan and hear from you. Father, we pray that you would guide us as to what to do and how to do it. Help us to embrace this journey remembering you are sovereign and do all things well. Be with us as we try to conceive. In Jesus' name. Amen.

God's Word

For I know the plans I have for you, declares the LORD, plans for welfare and not for evil, to give you a future and a hope.
Jeremiah 29:11 (ESV)

Miscarriage

Mother's Day was approaching. Kirey was going to be traveling home to New Jersey to celebrate with his mom and I was staying home in Maryland as my mom would be there. I was late. I felt strange and had noticed this feeling I had experienced many times before. THIS time, I wanted to test early so I could share it with him. I decided to take a pregnancy test. After taking so many pregnancy tests and getting false positives and the like, I had decreased the frequency of when I took them whether I was late or not.

    AT LAST, a positive pregnancy result! It was the Friday before Mother's Day and there could NOT have been a better time to learn that I was pregnant. The details were hazy, but, as I recall, I showed Kirey the test results before he left for his mother's and together, we rejoiced. It was FINALLY time. I mean, after all, we waited patiently (well, he did... not me) on the Lord and, FINALLY, He was answering. We didn't have time to really celebrate because Kirey was traveling. We knew we had time and we just needed to stay calm and keep the news to ourselves (yeah, ok). I managed to not die from excitement on Saturday. I really did think the excitement would kill me along with keeping it a secret. We talked throughout the days discussing and wondering all the things we normally would once we were pregnant.

How far along was I? When would the baby be born? Would it be a boy or a girl? Would we have twins? What would we name the child/children? I mean, seriously? At this point, we had not had any assisted fertility. We were just operating by faith; so, that was enough. Saturday was great. I hung out with family. I stayed silent. I talked to my husband by phone. I was happy. Who am I kidding? I was elated!

I was up early that Mother's Day Sunday. Literally, I laid in the bed just thinking about how I wish Kirey was home with me that day as I reflected on our FINALLY and planned for our family. We had expected it before but had not received a confirmation. I'd taken 3-4 tests (that's common when you're in shock, you know).

That morning, I sat up. Wait, what was that feeling? Wait! Whew! That was a sharp cramp! I had read and experienced a lot; so, I figured this pain was common.

Nothing like running to the bathroom first thing in the morning. I mean EVERYONE knows what that's like. Happens to me every day. But THIS day was different. Mother's Day 2008 was different. I jumped up to run to the bathroom and felt like I didn't make it. What in THE world? "I'm too old for this," I thought. As I looked down, it was the sight I did NOT want to see. Crushed. Dismayed. Angry. Hurt. Shattered. It's Sunday! It's Mother's Day! God, why would THIS be my plight?

It was a challenging day, to say the least. Finding hope, peace, strength, joy, and understanding was impossible for me. It was my husband who covered us in prayer. It was my husband who encouraged me in God's word (even when it was difficult to hear). It was my husband, who even in distance, was right there, praying me through. He reminded that we trust in the Lord: Psalm 20:7[7]. If you've experienced a miscarriage, you understand the pain and grief associated with it. It is my prayer; you will be encouraged in God's word. I pray that your husband will cover you in prayer and in God's word when you are unable. I pray you will TRUST IN THE LORD!

---

[7] Psalm 20:7 (KJV): Some trust in chariots, and some in horses: but we will remember the name of the Lord our God.

A Moment to H.O.P.E.

Have you experienced miscarriage? Do you know the feeling of despair, anguish, sorrow, or grief? As you think of your personal experience or thoughts surrounding miscarriage, share your thoughts in the space provided.

Reflections

_____

_____

_____

_____

_____

_____

_____

_____

_____

Prayer

Father, we have waited so long for answered prayer. Our hearts are broken by miscarriage. Our lives are changed forever because of this loss. Lord, please comfort us. Wrap your loving arms around us and comfort us. Lord, we are waiting on you. We wait for your healing. We wait for your peace. Be with us in this season. In Jesus' name. Amen.

God's Word

Some trust in chariots, and some in horses: but we will remember the name of the Lord our God.

Psalm 20:7 (KJV)

Honey, I'm So Sorry

I knew what had happened. I didn't rush to see the doctor. Honestly, I had this experience before, just not right after a positive test result. Crying hysterically, I called my husband and wept as I told him the news. The child I thought we would share with the world was no more. Our "FINALLY" had turned to "Why God? Why?"

Too often I felt like this. Whether there was a certainty or the lack of positive results, the inability to carry, the loss and the shame was debilitating. It was paralyzing. I was sick and tired of this feeling and it was getting harder to fight the powerful emotions that engulfed me.

"Honey, I'm sorry. I don't know what I did." How many times can you apologize? How many times do you feel like your body is a war zone and NOTHING will survive there? Can you REALLY be sorry for something you have no control over? Do you know what it feels like to have your body betray you?

Alone. Quiet. Silenced. Lonely. Angry. Abandoned. Ashamed. Inadequate.

Just some of the things I felt that Mother's Day. Yes, I was going to celebrate with my mother. All while wondering if I would ever have the opportunity to have a child that would celebrate with me. Would Mother's Day ever be different for me? Would it now be the curse of remembering this experience? So many questions and the only thing I could truly say is, "Honey, I am so sorry."

There are others that have shared their stories on web pages and blogs where TTC is common. The theme is the same. Women who are apologetic and ashamed of something we absolutely have no control over. I know, in the sovereignty of God, *if* it was His will that I carry that child or that you carried your child – He would have allowed it. However, in the sovereignty of God – He did not. So, my sorry is not for something I did. It is for something I didn't do. I didn't trust God more. I did not accept or embrace His plan for my life.

As I reflect on those regrets and apologies, I can encourage *YOU* to learn from me. As a believer, we are confident that God is for us and not against us. As women and men of God, we know that we are called to suffer for the sake of Christ. Somehow, when it came to *chasing rainbows,* I was unable to embrace that completely. I regret doubting God because it only added anguish. Now, I embrace God's plan for my life (even when it is difficult) and I urge you to do the same thing. I can hear one of my favorite hymns often as I fought to believe. We come this far by faith, trusting in God's Holy word. Trust in God's word. Walk by faith and do NOT doubt. You *ARE* loved by God.

A Moment to H.O.P.E.

Do you ever feel sorry for something you cannot change or control? Take a moment to write down your thoughts on the regret or apologies you can recall surrounding miscarriage. Whether you have apologized or felt apologetic, recognize that you, my sister, are not in control.

Reflections

_____

_____

_____

_____

_____

_____

_____

_____

Prayer

Father, I realize I am not in control of my life. Lord, you are the giver of life and I have been saturated with guilt and shame. I pray for strength and that you would free me from the feelings of guilt and shame. You are in control. I love you and I trust you. Thank you for allowing me access to prayer and the reminder that you alone are God. In Jesus' name. Amen.

God's Word

He heals the brokenhearted and binds up their wounds.
Psalm 147:3 (ESV)

Oh, No! Not Again!

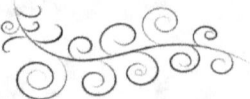

Many women share the story of multiple miscarriages. "I can't even count how many times I have cried or wanted to just give up." This is the same refrain from so many women on the TTC and fertility blogs. Women who are seeking help from strangers... looking to find others who can relate.

You hear people say, "Well, it's ok. After you have a miscarriage, it's easier to get pregnant." Who does that apply to? Who came up with that? Is that supposed to be comforting rhetoric? How many times have you thought to yourself, "Yeah, I just had a miscarriage that means next month will be better?" Or how many times have you thought, "This is getting harder and harder?" The positives are far and few between. Maybe they are just non-existent. For some women, there is no hope seen during the TTC journey. This pain – there is no comparison, no reward, no winners, just pain.

"Not again" is how I felt month after month and year after year. I didn't know grief could be this consistent. I laughed as I made that point; but, honestly, grief became my norm. I would bounce in and out of the stages of grief. Loss became a security blanket for me. I had become so used to the disappointment that I would condition myself for the failed attempt thinking I would be less devastated each month; but that did not happen. The devastation grew stronger.

Each month brought worries, pain, shame, doubt, fear, rejection, and grief specific to that month. It was sometimes accompanied by other sorrow and sometimes connected to the sorrows of another month. It depended on when it was and how many other things were happening. What I know for sure is this, multiple miscarriages do not make the loss easier to deal with. You just deal with it more frequently. I certainly did.

The more it happened, the more I prayed. I would search the word and pray God's word over my womb, over my life, over my future. I was able to cling to God's word often and I encourage you to, also. There are many prayers in the Bible about infertility. Infertility is NOT new to God. We saw it from the VERY beginning with Sarah. Numerous women in the Bible struggled to conceive. So, God is no stranger to our pain or our prayers.

A Moment to H.O.P.E.

Have you experienced multiple miscarriages? Do you find yourself saying, "Not again?" Take a moment and share your thoughts in the space provided and pray aloud the prayer that follows.

Reflections

_____

_____

_____

_____

_____

_____

_____

_____

Prayer

Lord, I admit I am tired. I am growing accustomed to this loss and I do not want to be numb to your presence in my life. Lord, I recognize that no matter how absent it feels you are; I understand that you are with me. You have a plan and you absolutely know what's best for me. Comfort me, Father, and give me peace. In Jesus' name. Amen.

God's Word

Be joyful in hope, patient in affliction, faithful in prayer.
Romans 12:12 (ESV)

Let's Give it a Try

"Let's give it a try," we said. We had thought about some of the methods we heard about and did research on what options were available to us. My husband and I had just moved to a new state and had a new Obstetrics and Gynecology medical team responsible for my treatment. They were excited about our possibilities and communicated to us that they had the perfect option for us to consider. They asked had we considered the option of assisted fertility, given it any thought, or if we had even tried it. Even eight years later, we were still in the "trust God" phase of this journey and were not completely sold on choosing assisted fertility as an option and a course of treatment.

They were Christian doctors. A husband and wife team, both committed to my care and the outcome we desired. They expressed such a bright outlook on what we were experiencing and what we could expect. My husband and I were pleased with them and on my first visit, I felt comfortable and at peace with the doctor and the possibilities he shared with me. We talked extensively about my history and about what he thought were the best options. We had not considered assisted fertility in the past.

Round one consisted of testing, planning, and discussing. Then Mother's Day came back around again. Not sure why, but I felt there must be something about Mother's Day that God seems to use to hold me hostage or to draw me to Him. I am sure that is a poor choice of words. At my core, I do not really believe it to be so. However, that is the best way I can explain it when I think of my *trying to conceive* and *Mother's Day experiences*.

It was Mother's Day weekend 2014. We had decided to give IUI a try. Why not? There was nothing to lose. Since it was determined there were no concerns to point to why we had not conceived; we felt this was a great option. We were heading to New Jersey that weekend; so, we knew we would be busy. That Saturday morning, we headed to our appointment and embarked on a new path on this journey toward *trying to conceive*.

I had such a great feeling that day. I just knew THIS was it. EVERYTHING was aligning. Everything seemed to be in place. We had relocated to a new state. We were in a new home (three times the size of our previous home) which seemed important since we were planning to start a family. We were in a new season of life. Why wouldn't THIS be the time?

We traveled from North Carolina to New Jersey discussing all the things we discussed Mother's Day Weekend 2008, six years prior. Which room would be the baby's? What color should we paint the room? We had chosen grey paint as we could use it no matter what the sex of the baby would be. WE had a plan. WE had a vision. WE had hope.

We prayed. We tried. We prayed. We waited. He prayed. I cried. Not yet. God said, "No!"

Oh, how sick and tired was I of hearing, "GOD SAID NO!"

The funny thing about God's 'no' was that it still had a resounding 'yes' each time. I am still unable to describe what this was like for me; however, I was not weary after experiencing God's 'no' on our first assisted fertility attempt. I was experiencing peace and hope that it was just a matter of time. As you journey through assisted fertility, I want to encourage you to speak life, sing praises, read God's word, and trust His hand even when you cannot trace it.

The sweet melody of *Great is Thy Faithfulness* resounds for me and I pray it will comfort you and give you hope. God's faithfulness is great, and God is good. (Lamentations 3:22-23[8])

---

[8] Lamentations 3:22-23 (ESV): The steadfast love of the Lord never ceases; his mercies never come to an end; they are new every morning; great is your faithfulness.

A Moment to H.O.P.E.

Have you experienced "THE WAIT"? If you know the journey of waiting after IUI or IVF, feel free to share your thoughts here and pray aloud the prayer that follows.

Reflections

_____

_____

_____

_____

_____

_____

_____

_____

_____

Prayer

God, we know you are sovereign and in the details. We know that you do ALL things well and that you are the giver and sustainer of life. God, we do not take it for granted that ALL power belongs to you. Father, you know the desires of our hearts. Help us to deal with the wait and give us peace, as we try, if we try, when we try, and after we try. In Jesus' name. Amen.

God's Word

The steadfast love of the Lord never ceases; his mercies never come to an end; they are new every morning; great is your faithfulness.
Lamentations 3:22-23 (ESV)

The Diagnosis

After months of not having the results we desired and multiple doctor's appointments, we started to hear the disturbing curiosity of the doctors. "We are not quite sure what happened *this* time." "We see this kind of thing all the time." "Let's run some tests," they said. "Have you and your husband ever had assisted fertility in the past (I knew we had already covered this)?" "We want to do a series of tests to make sure everything is as it should be," they said. "Let's see what we have going on and we can decide what alternatives we have."

After months of testing and more testing as well as a few failed attempts, they decided on a diagnosis. The diagnosis was "Unexplained infertility". According to the National Institutes of Health (NIH), *"When the results of a standard infertility evaluation are normal, practitioners assign a diagnosis of unexplained infertility. Although estimates vary, the likelihood that all such test results for an infertile couple are normal (i.e., that the couple has unexplained infertility) is approximately 15% to 30%*[9].

---

[9] Standard treatment better than potential alternative for unexplained infertility. (2015, September 24). Retrieved from https://www.nih.gov/news-events/news-releases/standard-treatment-better-potential-alternative-unexplained-infertility

That was the answer! After years of not conceiving and/or carrying a child to term, they FINALLY figured out what was wrong! Do you sense the sarcasm here? My husband and I came up with the same thing without an advanced medical degree or the thousands and thousands of dollars we spent on that diagnosis.

After meeting with our regular team, all our records were forwarded to the specialist for further review and we were referred there for consultation on more advanced treatment. The question we had was, how do you treat something you have no awareness of? If the infertility is unexplained and we've tried all the things suggested, what was the point? We scheduled the appointment. We attended the appointment. We decided.

This was a period of confusion for me and a time when we rested in our knowledge of God and who He was. We spoke God's word over our lives. We prayed God's plan for our lives, and we walked in the ordered steps God had for us. *God, our lives are entrusted in you. Show us which way to go.* (Psalm 143:8[10]) My husband and I encourage couples who are experiencing confusion and uncertainty on this journey, to meditate on God's word, pray and wait for God to answer. Even in the midst of our chaos, God is still with us.

---

[10] Psalm 143:8 (NIV): Let the morning bring me word of your unfailing love, for I have put my trust in you. Show me the way I should go, for to you I entrust my life.

A Moment to H.O.P.E.

Have you had experience with "unexplained infertility"? Do you feel like you were out of options yet still directed to consider more? Think about this discussion and share your thoughts. Once you are finished, read aloud the prayer that follows.

Reflections

_____

_____

_____

_____

_____

_____

Prayer

Father, I know you indeed know the diagnosis. There is nothing that escapes you; and while it is unexplainable to man, it is clearly understood by you. In the sovereignty of your will for our lives, we pray for peace. God help us to trust your answer and your will and plan for our lives. In Jesus' name. Amen.

God's Word

Let the morning bring me word of your unfailing love, for I have put my trust in you. Show me the way I should go, for to you I entrust my life.
Psalm 143:8 (NIV)

The Prognosis

We decided to consult with one of the top-rated reproductive centers, with the largest cutting-edge facility in the state of North Carolina. During the visit, it did not take long. Upon speaking with the doctor, we knew immediately we were in the right place. The doctor reviewed our history and spoke with us clearly sharing statistics, options, and a well thought out assisted fertility treatment plan.

We had questions. We needed answers. And so, we asked, and he answered. The doctor was extremely knowledgeable and gave very candid explanations. After a thorough discussion, he offered us the options. Together, we left knowing our decision. The doctor had a very aggressive and immediate plan. Considering, at this point, I was classified advanced maternal age, he advised us we had no time to wait.

The prognosis was that there is nothing wrong. We only know that based on my age, we didn't have a lot of time. I mean seriously, what they were telling us was that we should invest... wait... *waste* (according to how I felt about it) about $30,000 on a chance to produce nothing. I mean, the odds were all stacked against us. And somehow that seemed like a great idea to the doctor. It was difficult to hear the plan and receive it with hope when it was presented and peppered with doubt and low chance of success statistics. Although, we knew we wanted a family, we were committed to focusing on what God's will and plan for our lives was if we did NOT have children naturally.

This may not be our story alone. This may be *your* story or the story of someone you know. This may also be the story of the many women I sat near quietly as we all suffered in silence on this journey. This *IS* the story of women around the globe. Each time I hear a woman share her story, or a couple share their story, I am reminded of the pain I felt each time I thought about how my purpose and promise were tied to parenting. The myth that I believed for as long as I can remember.

According to research and our experience, unexplained infertility is typically treated empirically. The treatment plan is determined based on the experience of the medical professional and, of course, a little guess work and the woman's/couple's willingness to explore various treatment options. We often laugh and say, that's why they call it "practicing medicine". Whatever the case, after multiple miscarriages, extended fails at attempts to conceive and unsuccessful cycles of TTC using assisted fertility, the prognosis for us, was not good.

While the thought of this prognosis seemed gloom and I felt it was not good, there was one thing I knew with great certainty: God was STILL great! Before I was even born God knew me and had a plan for my life. The myth that my worth was tied into motherhood, was integral in causing me to feel depressed and unworthy. BUT GOD... (those two words and six letters are always life changing and a point of redirection, focus and promise), who loved me more than I could imagine, reminded me through His word that He created me with a purpose, fearfully and wonderfully (Psalm 139:14[11]) and no prognosis, diagnosis, or medical report could thwart His purpose, promise and plan for my life. Whew, take a break and reflect on that verse. The sovereign God of the universe has a plan for you, and you are fearfully and wonderfully made. The journey of chasing rainbows will NEVER change that.

---

[11] Psalm 139:14 (NIV): I praise you because I am fearfully and wonderfully made; your works are wonderful, I know that full well.

A Moment to H.O.P.E.

Women who suffer in silence because of this prognosis are often lonely and isolated. They feel their worth is tied to conceiving, giving birth and motherhood. That is a lie. We were created fearfully and wonderfully, and we can rejoice knowing that God is ALWAYS with us. If you are familiar with this prognosis, what are your thoughts within your own experience? Take a moment to share your thoughts and reflect on your personal journey and pray aloud or within the prayer that follows.

Reflections

_____

_____

_____

_____

_____

_____

Prayer

God, we recognize that while others are deeming this unexplained and are practicing medicine, you Jesus are the Master physician. You are the one who heals, restores and creates life. YOU alone are the Giver of Life. God there is nothing too hard for you. As we walk through this journey, if feelings of hopelessness and grief overwhelm us, please give us peace. If we get distracted by the lies the enemy tells and lose sight of who we are in you, remind us through your word that we are fearfully and wonderfully made. In Jesus' name. Amen.

God's Word

I praise you because I am fearfully and wonderfully made; your works are wonderful, I know that full well.
Psalm 138:14 (NIV)

It's Not Happening...Now What?

I never had the opportunity to share this journey with others experiencing it. I knew women who had miscarried, but some of them went on to have children. I am not downplaying the pain and despair these women experienced, but the longing I had, I felt that I was unable to share. I chose not to share it. Maybe, it was based on the space I was in. Maybe, I just did not know what to say without sounding insensitive to what they experienced. Maybe, the opportunity did not present itself. Maybe, I was ashamed and felt guilt and the thought of sharing that sorrow didn't seem to offer any relief.

When making the decision to turn down the treatment plan offered, I felt good about it, THAT DAY. We really went before the Lord and prayed about it before deciding. We had been taking it before the Lord, long before we were faced with deciding; but additional prayer seemed necessary with such a life-changing decision (I was asking God for a sign because I just wanted to be sure). Praying without ceasing (1 Thessalonians 5:17[12]), isn't that

---

[12] 1 Thessalonians :17 (KJV): Pray without ceasing.

what we are instructed to do? We knew that the efforts we had made prior, while God allowed it, neither one of us were certain that God ordained it or ordered our steps. This time, it was critical that we waited for the Lord to answer before we made the decision.

We made the decision knowing, at that moment and in that season, it would not happen. We had to determine our "next" steps. For my husband, he had faith that whatever God's will was for our lives, would be done. For me, I knew I had to fight. I felt numb. I was angry. Each day that I reflected on the decision we made, was another day of immeasurable grief.

What do you do when you experience immeasurable grief, heartache, and pain? You pray, seek the Lord, and plead with Him to comfort you and give you peace. This was a pivotal point in my faith walk, in my mental health, and in my future. I had to choose. I chose hope, even when I did not know where it was coming from. Each day, I focused on something to be grateful for outside of what I was feeling. Some days I was successful, and some days were challenging. If there is anything, I can say to encourage you, I will say this, read God's word, listen to songs of praise, pray, and when you cannot pray... remember that the Holy Spirit is interceding for you. God's plan for you is good. It stretches beyond what our plans and expectations are and His will for your life is good and perfect.

A Moment of H.O.P.E.

Are you in your "now what" season? Are you wondering what to do now that all the options are off the table and you have finally come to realizing that it's not happening or just not happening yet? Are you feeling numb to the decision God made for your life in this season? Take a moment and write down your thoughts as you think about this season and read aloud or within the prayer that follows.

Reflections

_____

_____

_____

_____

_____

_____

_____

Prayer

Father, we want to trust you. I prayed for you to open my womb. I prayed that I would not be barren. Your Will is best for us and there is nothing we desire more than to be safely in your Will. God, our hearts long for this child we desire. Please align our desires with yours and give us peace. In Jesus' name. Amen.

God's Word

The heart of man plans his way, but the Lord establishes his steps.

Proverbs 16:9 (ESV)

Look Who's Pregnant Now!

It was some years ago and I was sitting at work (well, home in my bedroom/office or "boffice" as my brother calls it) completing some tasks. It was early in the day and I remember, like it was yesterday. It must have been one of those emotionally charged days. Of course, I was unaware of the emotions I was feeling until what I am about to share happened.

    I received a text from someone as I was working, sharing their good news. I reached out to them earlier that week to see how they were doing, as they had been on my heart and mind. The text I received read, "I'm pregnant! Yes, we are expecting, baby number three!" I responded with pleasantries and before I knew it, I was in a full-blown breakdown. Oh, I am not exaggerating. Some of the hardest days I endured were the *Look Who's Pregnant Now* days.

    I screamed so loud I thought the neighbors would call 911. I called one of my sister-in-Christ in complete hysteria and crying frantically. She couldn't calm me. She couldn't hear me, and I couldn't stop. I was able to articulate what was happening (a little) through my violent sobs and she began to pray. After we hung up, it was evident, I needed to take the day off. I was unable to self-regulate enough to work and managing my emotions had quickly become, a thing of the past.

After calling and explaining everything to my husband who replied, "I hate that for you", I hung up and cried some more. I cannot recall doing anything that day but cry. I was sick. I was angry. I was feeling emotions I did not know I had. I was ANGRY WITH GOD! There was nothing God could do for me. I was alone in that moment. Everyone around me was blessed but me (the lies the enemy had begun telling me). Although I knew this wasn't the case, it sure felt like it. In this moment, I felt rejected by God and worthless.

For weeks, maybe months, I struggled with those feelings. I couldn't escape it. I couldn't share it. I couldn't shake it. I smiled. I worked. I held back tears. I kept moving like nothing was wrong until one day. I realized; I was sick. I had a problem. I was suffering from inconsolable grief and unmanageable depression. Something was missing and I could NOT accept God's will for my life in that season.

This was one of the most difficult and painful seasons on this journey of chasing rainbows through barren land. I was completely lost. I was inconsolable. I had wavered faith, righteous indignation (how could I NOT be pregnant?), and fear that I would NEVER be able to trust God again. I was spiraling and it was happening quickly.

My encouragement to you is to get help. If you feel yourself spiraling or feeling any of the powerful emotions I have described, do NOT wait to get help. Don't dismiss your feelings as invalid or silly. This journey is traumatic, and trauma should be treated by a Licensed Professional. Cling to the cross and remember that *"all things work together for good to those who love God"* (Romans 8:28 NKJV). I encourage you to give voice to the silence, be heard so you can be healed.

A Moment of H.O.P.E.

If you have experienced this overwhelming grief when learning of a friend, family member or even a stranger's pregnancy, then you may know what inconsolable grief or depression feels like. Take a moment and share your thoughts and personal experience in the space provided. After reflecting on your own inconsolable grief and/or experience, pray aloud or within the prayer that follows.

Reflections

_____

_____

_____

_____

_____

_____

_____

_____

Prayer

Father, forgive me for thinking more highly of myself than I should. God, I recognize that when I act like that, I am saying that you are making a mistake. I am measuring their gift against the giver and I certainly do not want to do that. God, help me to genuinely be happy for others. Lord, help me to come alongside them and love them. God remove the spirit of jealousy or envy that may take residence and saturate me with your peace. Lord, give me wisdom and guidance as to who to seek for help and help me give voice to my silence. In Jesus' name. Amen.

God's Word

And we know that for those who love God all things work together for good, for those who are called according to his purpose.

Romans 8:28 (ESV)

Who Can I Talk To?

It was a Sunday afternoon after church. We had been invited to a birthday party. The child was turning one and I knew we had to be there. They were like family and I couldn't keep hiding (the depression had me self-isolating to avoid people noticing my change in countenance). My husband was not feeling well; so, I decided to go alone. It was just a birthday party. I would be alright. Or so I thought.

The week before, I came downstairs to greet my husband when he got home from work. I said to him, "I think it's time I get help. I need to talk with someone." Literally, you would think I told him I hit the Powerball numbers. He hugged me and said, "Thank you." My sister-in-Christ had been researching therapists in the area for me since that awful breakdown. I had recently finished my coursework to become a Licensed Professional Counselor and the only requirement was an internship which I had been searching diligently for throughout that year. I had the list of counselors that I could see, but I never called. I waited. I procrastinated. I thought, maybe, this feeling would pass. I figured, I had overcome it in the past, this couldn't be much different.

At the birthday party, I stood in the corner, almost by the door. My emotions were unstable, and I had not realized it until I was at the party. I stood by the door talking to friends to keep me distracted. All I remember saying is, "Hey, is there someone you can refer me to in the area? I need to talk to someone." They leaned closer to me as if I would say more. I stated that I could not talk about it. I just need to get the information so I could start seeing a therapist. In that moment, I found myself right back on the verge of that mental meltdown. This was getting frequent and dangerous. In the past, I had experienced emotions surrounding my journey through barren land (as I have often referred to it in my mind), but they were more calculated and controlled.

A few days later, I reached out to my friend (while sitting on the couch on the brink of a breakdown) and she shared the information of the therapist she recommended. As God would have it, it was the same person my sister-in-Christ found during her search of therapists in my area. I made my appointment that day and within a few days, I FINALLY had someone to talk to. I was giving voice to the silence in hopes that the chains of infertility would be loosed, and I would be free of the pain, anger, fear, and powerful emotions that had imprisoned me.

If you have been on this journey any length of time and you are anything like me, there are very few opportunities to give your silence a voice. Everyone around me was having children. The people who were not having children either didn't have the desire or were waiting on marriage before starting a family. The stigma associated with infertility speaks volumes. Everyone hears it and no one wants to speak about it. I thought I was alone. I felt alone. I was alone. Surrounded by people, yet very much ALONE.

I did have opportunities to speak to people. Most times, I talked to my sister-in-law. Seldom would I speak about my hurt to anyone who was single; I felt it would be selfish to share my desire for a child knowing they had a desire for marriage. This was a burden I really felt I needed to carry alone. Although my husband was there, I never felt he understood what I was experiencing. His faith in God was so strong. He wanted God's will for our lives no matter what that meant and, to be honest, I wanted MY will for my life. I wanted children. I wanted a family and what God gave me, just wasn't enough.

So, as a Christian, who could I talk to? With whom would I share my ugly truth? The truth that I was angry with God, did not like or trust His plan, and felt He was dealing with me bitterly for whatever reason. What Christian would be comfortable with that discussion or comforting to me? Afterall, we are supposed to trust God's plan, but I struggled.

I know I was not alone because I have since talked to a *few* women who shared parts of their story involving infertility. I have not heard details and I have never thought or felt anyone I knew understood or could relate to what I was experiencing. Maybe it was ignorance. Maybe it was truth, but it was my perception. Thus, it was my reality.

Calling the therapist was one of the *best* things I could have done. She was amazing and she could relate to what I was experiencing. I had no clue how God would work that in my favor, but I knew that He was present even in that decision. After about 5 – 6 sessions, I felt a lot better. She asked me something that was critical to how I shaped my desire. Why did I want to be a mother? That question changed me and was the catalyst for all the decisions that came next.

If I could encourage you in anything it would be to know that you are not alone. God is always with you and the Lord hears your prayers. (Isaiah 41:10 NIV)

A Moment of H.O.P.E.

Have you ever been a prisoner to your silence? Do you know what it is like to be stuck in Barren Land with no voice and just the vision of what appears to be eyes of judgement? Take a moment to share your thoughts on suffering in silence and then pray aloud or within the prayer that follows.

Reflections

_____

_____

_____

_____

_____

_____

_____

_____

Prayer

Lord, I know that your word says, come to me, all ye who are weary and heavy laden. God, I am weary. I am heavy laden. I feel alone and I feel that there is no one who understands what I am experiencing. God, I need to hear from you. I need you to incline your ear and hear the prayers of my heart. Lord, you are in control and you have the final say. Please Jesus, I do not want to suffer in silence. Give voice to my silence and grant me peace. In Jesus' name. Amen.

God's Word

So do not fear, for I am with you; do not be dismayed, for I am your God. I will strengthen you and help you; I will uphold you with my righteous right hand

Isaiah 41:10 (NIV)

No, Not Tonight

Is infertility ruining your sex life? Is intimacy lost?

Women and couples struggling with infertility often don't have an outlet and, therefore, the suffering is in silence. So, how do you learn how to cope if there is no one to talk to? How do you manage to get through the nights of intimacy and days when your cycle shows up? How do you look at your husband and desire intimacy when each time you expect intimacy to yield fertility, disappointment abound?

Often women who suffer with fertility issues also struggle with the desire to be intimate. This is common for so many reasons. Infertility challenges cause emotional issues and affect a woman's ability to feel whole. In my experience, infertility may cause women to feel devalued and broken.

For Christians, we believe what God's word says about childbirth. As women, we were created to bring forth life. As husbands, it is a blessing to plant seeds that yield life. The Bible says, *"blessed is a man whose quiver is full,"* (Psalm 127:5). The Bible instructs us to, *"be fruitful and multiply,"* (Genesis 1:28). To know the body was created for something it doesn't do truly hurts and is sometimes difficult to comprehend and accept. It is almost like the body is rejecting you. How do you honor your body when you feel your body is dishonoring you? Wives struggle with intimacy. It isn't intentional. It's unconscious and unmanageable at times. What do you do when you desire to satisfy your husband, yet the pain that saturates your heart paralyzes you? What do you do when your sex life is suffering during your struggle?

- **Pray!** Ask God to help you trust His plan for your life. Jeremiah 29:11
- **Trust!** God's plan for your life is greater than what you can imagine. Proverbs 3:5-6
- **Know!** Know your body is a temple. It belongs to the Lord! Do that which would please God with it. 1 Corinthians 6:19
- **Imagine!** Imagine what it would be like to be in the will of God, honoring Him in ALL that you do. Luke 22:42
- **Honor!** Honor your vows to your husband being mindful that your body is not your own. 1 Corinthians 7:4
- **Love!** Love your husband. Remember, he is not the enemy. Your loss is his loss. You are ONE! Ephesians 5:22-25
- **Surrender!** Surrender your plan for your life to God's plan for you. Knowing His plan is much greater! Galatians 2:20

Intimacy is an important part of your marriage. It is critical, and God created sex for marriage. My pre-marriage counselor told us that God created sex for recreation, procreation, and communication during our pre-marriage counseling sessions. Just because one component is missing doesn't mean fulfilling the others are not necessary. Embrace your spouse. Embrace God's plan and get ready to embark on the best sex and intimacy you've had. FREE YOUR MIND… AND GREAT SEX WILL FOLLOW!

Intimacy was challenging at times because I had a quid pro quo mindset regarding it. I really felt sex should lead to conception and when that did not happen, since my husband was tangible (or maybe not during those times ☺), I rejected him based on my frustration with God.

If you experience challenges with intimacy based on a quid pro quo mindset, I encourage you to surrender your will to the Lord. Sex is a mandate and withholding is simply disobedience to God. If you consistently experience challenges with intimacy, I encourage you to pray fervently, ask God to change your heart and seek professional help. Working with a therapist helped me to identify what was at the core of those feelings. My negative cognitions were shifted, and intimacy was restored! HALLELUJAH!

A Moment of H.O.P.E.

Has infertility affected your intimacy? If you are familiar with this area and know it as a part of your journey, take a moment and reflect on your thoughts and write them in the space provided. Then take a few moments to pray aloud or within the prayer that follows.

Reflections

_____

_____

_____

_____

_____

_____

_____

_____

Prayer

Father, please strengthen your daughter. Comfort her and speak life into her dead situation. Restore her anew and allow her to love herself and her husband in ways she has never known. Bind them together with bonds that cannot be broken. Give them fresh ways to love one another as they learn to love and trust you. Ignite a fire in them that causes their passion to burn for one another and be glorified. In Jesus' name. Amen.

God's Word

The husband should fulfill his marital duty to his wife, and likewise the wife to her husband.
1 Corinthians 7:3 (NIV)

I'm Not Woman Enough

"*Be fruitful and multiply.*" That is what it says in Genesis 1:28 (KJV). From the very beginning, God called us to bear children. This is where I struggled as a Christian woman. "*Blessed is a man whose quiver is full*" is how it is written in Psalm 127:5 (NIV). What should I take from that? When I reflect on God's promise from the very beginning and blessed is a man whose quiver is full, I focus on there being something wrong with me because my husband's quiver is empty. What happened to me that I cannot do the very thing God called me to do? Why is it that I blame myself when I have absolutely no control over the matter?

    I remember someone coming up to me in church, almost pushing to make their way to me. They finally reached me and said, "Congratulations!" With a puzzled look on my face, I responded with a short, "On?" They said, "On being pregnant. I heard you were pregnant." Without hesitance, my response was, "Oh, I am not pregnant." To which they responded, "Oh, I thought you had something to be happy about," as they laughed and walked away.

    How should I have felt? What did not having a child say about me? What did struggling to conceive say about me? What did being unable to carry full-term say about me? What should I have said to her response?

Sunday mornings were some of the most difficult days for me. It's where I learned what not to say to women and people, in general, for that matter. Words began to have more meaning to me as a result of this trial. I learned to believe that, maybe, just maybe, I was not woman enough. We must do better and ensure this is not how we are causing other women to feel. Why is it so difficult to realize the pain words cause? As a woman, I've learned to encourage women in all seasons. The silent suffering screams loudly and I am sensitive to those screams.

It was Mother's Day (again it seems to ALWAYS be Mother's Day when these life altering events happen). Mother's Day at church was typically uneventful. Normally, an all-women's choir would sing and a few mothers would get up and speak. This day, this day was different. It was the day I cemented that I was not woman enough.

"I want all the mothers to stand." "I want all the grandmothers to stand." "I want all the mothers-to-be to stand." "Everyone else remain seated." That was the part. It was the "everyone else remain seated" part. This day, it seemed that almost EVERY.WOMAN.IN.THE.CHURCH was standing. I didn't fit into any category to stand. So, I was sitting, heartbroken, holding back tears, in paralyzing pain, shame and despair.

For the first time that I can remember, I felt something worse than feeling invisible. I felt that EVERYONE could see me. In that moment, EVERYONE knew I was NOT a mother. It didn't matter to them that I had been a foster parent (of course, I could have stood for that). What it felt like to me is that in a land full of women who were mothers – I.WAS.NOT.

For too long, not being able to carry a child to term caused me to feel inadequate, weak, defective, insignificant, inferior, hopeless, and invisible. Praise be to God! I now know those feelings were a lie. God's word gave me strength and reminded me that I belong to God. That meant, I was enough! I was created in the image of God. I am an image bearer and those negative emotions which paralyzed my thinking are cognitive distortions. They are not true. Motherhood does not define me. Even without giving birth God has purpose, promise and a plan for my life and yours. I implore you to shift your thoughts if you are feeling any of the things above. You are an image bearer and you are enough.

A Moment of H.O.P.E

If you have experienced the feeling of "not being woman enough", inadequate or any other adaptation of lies from the enemy as a result of your inability to conceive, take a moment and share your thoughts in the space provided and then pray aloud or within the prayer that follows.

Reflections

_____

_____

_____

_____

_____

_____

_____

_____

Prayer

Father, I know your word says, I am fearfully and wonderfully made. You have a plan for my life. God you are a good, good, father and to believe that something is wrong with me is to believe you have failed. You do not fail, and I trust your plan. Give me the strength to do so even when I cannot find the strength. Surely, I have difficulty believing I am enough, and I have value. Some days, I feel defective and unworthy. Some days, I am ashamed of the way my body has rejected me. Oh Lord, I thank you for your grace, mercy and protection and I need you to help me see the value you have placed on me outside of motherhood. God, unveil my purpose and give me strength and peace. In Jesus' name. Amen.

God's Word

My grace is sufficient for you, for my power is made perfect in weakness. Therefore, I will boast all the more gladly of my weaknesses, so that the power of Christ may rest upon me. For the sake of Christ, then, I am content with weaknesses, insults, hardships, persecutions, and calamities. For when I am weak, then I am strong.

2 Corinthians 12:9-10 (ESV)

Fault Doesn't Matter

One of the first things people ask is whose fault is it? Did you both get tested? Yes, I encountered people who really did have the audacity to ask personal questions like this. What is it they really want to know and why does it matter? They say it as if fault changes a diagnosis or helps couples cope with the devastation known as infertility.

I think we are naturally conditioned to place blame. But what does that mean? Does that mean we determine fault, assign blame, and then everything will be better? If I began to point fingers at my husband, will I, then, be able to conceive? If he pointed the blame to me, will I, then, be able to conceive?

It's absurd to think that question has any value. It's on the blogs all the time. When you read the blogs, you see conversations about blame and who's at fault. Is that a thing in marriage? It made me sad for people who did not have "unexplained infertility", because this allowed them to potentially harbor feelings of anger or resentment toward their spouse. This blaming mindset was a catalyst for conflict. This mindset causes couples to give up, to divorce and to lose sight of the love they once shared.

I have heard individuals discuss blame, mainly in the absence of the other spouse. Personally, I think it is disrespectful.

Whether it is a condition of the husband or the wife, I find the conversation tasteless and without regard. Maybe because, personally, I felt afraid that my husband would not want to stay with me if I could not give him a child. So, in my mind, fault *did* matter. But in the sovereignty of God, I realized there was absolutely nothing either of us could do. God alone was the giver of life. It's not *my* fault. It's not *his* fault. It's not *OUR* fault.

Over the years, I have heard and known of people who have conceived in the most unusual of circumstances. People with tubal ligations, vasectomies, a twisted uterus, actively taking birth control, and many other obvious reasons *not* to conceive – conceive. God works miracles in the lives of so many where fertility is concerned. We see it on the news, and we hear of it through others. Still people want to know, whose fault is it. God IS the giver and creator of life and therein lies the answer. This is the will of God for my life and fault is not even a consideration.

Feeling defective was common for me throughout this season. With each failed attempt, miscarriage or TTC cycle, I felt broken. I am grateful for God's word that reminded me of how wonderfully made I am in Christ and that I was skillfully crafted into a work of art by a divine potter. (Isaiah 64:8[13])

---

[13] Isaiah 64:8 (NIV): Yet you, LORD, are our Father. We are the clay, you are the potter; we are all the work of your hand.

A Moment of H.O.P.E

Have you struggled with fault, guilt, shame or blame? Today, remember that you do not have the power to be at fault and you do not have the authority to place blame. God alone is sovereign, and He does all things well. Take a moment and write down your thoughts and reflections. Once you have done so, pray this prayer of comfort that follows.

Reflections

_____

_____

_____

_____

_____

_____

_____

Prayer

Father, I am tired of blame being a factor. I know that you are in control and there is no one who can change your will and/or plan for my life. Help me to respond to those who ask that question in love. Teach me to let my light shine. Whatever your will and plan is for my life, show me how to walk in it with peace. I need you to strengthen me for this journey, Father. In Jesus' name. Amen.

God's Word

Yet you, LORD, are our Father. We are the clay, you are the potter; we are all the work of your hand.

Isaiah 64:8 (NIV)

What Do You Say?

Sunday mornings (during worship), Thursday evenings (during choir rehearsal) and every family or church event you can think of were especially hard for me. Once we said, "I do", the question of when we would start a family or something close to that was all we heard. It outnumbered, "How are you?" "How are things?" "What are you into?" And all the other pleasantry related questions.

Initially, we both replied with the simple, "Oh, we're working on it" or "it's not for a lack of trying" with a laugh and a nod. That was normal. It was acceptable. It was fine. But as more time passed, the more invasive the questions became.

It became harder and harder to respond. Then it was difficult to respond with a Christ-centered response. After all, what makes us think we have the right to ask people such personal questions? Maybe we allow ourselves to be too familiar with people. Maybe we give explanations to people about things they do not have a need-to-know. Maybe we should exercise a little more privacy. Maybe.

Sure, I have wanted to ask others if they planned to start a family. I've wondered how many children they would like or how many MORE children they would like. However, because of my own experience and the emotions these questions evoke, I silence my curiosity and pray God's will for their lives and mine.

After years of asking, I realized my answer changed. Did it change because I wanted to conform? Did I want people to not feel sorry for me? Did it change because I knew what I wanted? Had I made up a story in my mind that I was comfortable with? The answers varied from day-to-day, month-to-month, year-to-year, and season-to-season. One thing I knew for sure; I was tired of the questions and I was tired of figuring out how I felt in the moment they were asked.

It's been thirteen years. Finally, I know what to say. My answer: "Well, only God knows." And *that*, my friends, is true. ONLY. GOD. KNOWS.

Waiting on God can be challenging. We do so not knowing what the outcome will be and wondering if God will answer the way we want. Often, I yielded to the Psalm as reading and praying through them gave me encouragement through waiting. I encourage you during this season, pray and read through the Psalm, it's where I learned how to wait.

A Moment to H.O.P.E.

Have you struggled with how to answer the questions about your desire for a child? Take a moment and write down your thoughts and reflections. Remember you get to choose your response and are not obligated to offer an explanation. There is complete freedom in knowing that.

Reflections

_____

_____

_____

_____

_____

_____

_____

_____

Prayer

Father, we know you alone have the answer to these questions. we have no clue when or if; but you know God. Help me to be confident in my response which is clearly, 'it is in the Lord's hands' and help me to wait on You trusting in your plan for our lives. In Christ's name, I pray. Amen.

God's Word

But they that wait upon the Lord, shall renew their strength; they shall mount up with wings like eagles; they shall run and not be weary; they shall walk and not faint.

Isaiah 40:31 (ESV)

When is Enough, Enough?

The day we sat in the office listening to the plans of the doctor and the odds which were stacked so high against us, we needed to decide. Had we done enough? And what does that even mean? What does "doing enough" look like? Did we try everything? Did we exhaust all our options? Should we consider everything they were proposing? What should we do? Did we really know if we had done enough?

The doctor was not confident it would work. The odds, he quoted, were really stacked against us. He never even suggested we position ourselves for the best chance to conceive. Yet, when we began asking questions, we knew, at that moment, we had done enough. Was it enough at that time? Was it enough in that season? Well, that wasn't as clear as I desired in that moment. However, for sure, I thought it was ENOUGH!

Enough will look different for everyone. I met women in waiting rooms who thought they had enough until they had a glimpse of hope. Some couples thought they had done enough until they learned of scholarships available for treatment. Some couples thought they had enough until they had new insurance coverage which now afforded them the opportunity to try fertility treatments, they couldn't consider before. For them, enough changed when opportunity changed. So, was it *really* enough?

In my situation, we knew we had to wait on the Lord and trust His plan for our lives. We knew we *did not* have the power to change God's plan. We decided that it was finally time to let go of the alternatives and trust God for His will. If I am honest, my husband always felt that way, but he wanted me to be satisfied. So, he allowed me to go through the motions as he prayed, waited, and trusted God.

Weighing the options was difficult individually and as a couple. Sometimes, we agreed and sometimes we had varying opinions. No matter what we were weighing, what odds were against us or what things were in our favor, we were sure of one thing. God was sovereign, we would seek him until he answered, and we would not move until God gave us clarity. We agreed on wanting God's will for our lives and nothing more. We found solace in Matthew 26:39[14] and not in our own will.

---

[14] Matthew 26:39 (NIV): Going a little farther, he fell with his face to the ground and prayed, "My Father, if it is possible, may this cup be taken from me. Yet not as I will, but as you will."

A Moment of H.O.P.E

Are you struggling with knowing when enough is enough? Are you torn with making decisions to use assisted fertility treatments? I encourage you to stop for a moment. Ask God for guidance. He will order your steps and He alone can help you. Take a moment and write down your thoughts and reflections in the space provided. Consider what you have already done on this journey and then meditate on the words of the prayer that follow.

Reflections

_____

_____

_____

_____

_____

_____

Prayer

Father, I stretch my hands to thee. No other help I know. God, we are uncertain as to what direction to go. We realize you are fully in control and no matter what decision we make, without it being Your will, we do not want it. Help us to be patient and trust your plan for our lives. In Christ's name, we pray. Amen.

God's Word

Not my will, but thine be done.
Luke 22:42b (NIV)

Alternatives to Natural Childbirth

A few months after hearing the plan of the doctor, we attended an adoption conference. We had already considered foster care and after the information session, we knew that God had not called us to that. The adoption conference was different. The speaker gave a riveting explanation about why we should adopt. He gave the reference as to how we are adopted by Christ and drew a compelling parallel as to the significance of adoption in the church.

At that point, we knew we would consider adoption. It was the alternative to childbirth. After years of talking about adoption and how I wanted to consider it, my husband came to me to discuss that consideration. What he said offended me. Once I reflected on the discussion, I realized it was not what he said that offended me, but it was the *truth* in what he said. "I think adoption would be great for us. My only fear is, if we did it, you still may not be happy." Whew! How could he say that to me? He was right. That was MY truth.

The answer I came up with came from the question the therapist asked (referenced in previous chapter). It was not that I wanted to be a mother as much as I wanted to *have* a baby. I wanted to carry a child in my womb. Our child. A child created out of our love and union. I wanted to BE pregnant and to feel the flutter of the movements in my belly. I wanted to know the experience of childbirth and everything that came with it, swollen ankles, and all! There was truth and validity to his statement and that broke my heart. My answer was shallow. But it was mine.

Years have passed, and we have been more immersed in the adoption culture. We still talk about it; but, like anything else, we consider, if we do not hear from God, it's not an option for us. *"For we walk by faith [and] not by sight."* (2 Corinthians 5:7 NKJV)

Fostering and adopting are two viable options to consider. At a young age, I always wanted to foster and/or adopt after my first foster child. What changed my mind? The shame of my personal fertility issues paralyzed me. Instead of remembering that adoption was one of my first options, I allowed shame to make it my last and something I was grossly embarrassed to consider.

I met Dunia when she was a teenager. God positioned us to meet and immediately, I knew she was special. After a long process, I was granted custody of her and our lives were forever changed. To me, she will ALWAYS be "mama's baby". To her, I will always be "Ma". I always planned to have more foster children or adopt; however, the shame of my journey through Barren Land robbed me of that. I want to encourage you to consider the options. We are adopted by Christ and God calls us to look after the orphaned.

A Moment to H.O.P.E.

If you are torn on considering alternatives to natural childbirth, I encourage you to do your research. I pray you will take time to learn more about your personal options and what they mean for you and your family. Reflect on your thoughts on this topic as you write them in the space provided. Once you are done, join me in praying for alternatives to natural childbirth that may be best for you and your husband.

Reflections

_____

_____

_____

_____

_____

_____

Prayer

Father, we do not want to do anything outside of your will. We want to know that you are with us, for us, guiding us and that we are safely tucked in your will. Lord, if you have a plan of parenting for us outside of natural childbirth, I pray you will reveal it in a manner that it is clearly you. Lord, help us to not be distracted by our own personal desires. Help us to be obedient to your will for our lives and show us which way to go. In Jesus's name. Amen.

God's Word

For you did not receive the spirit of slavery to fall back into fear, but you have received the Spirit of adoption as sons, by whom we cry, "Abba! Father!"
Romans 8:15 (ESV)

My Marriage is Hurting

My husband is an incredibly kind man. The kind of guy that loves beyond measures and without hesitation or boundaries. He loves me in season and out of season, but that isn't the story for everyone. Here's a scenario I pray you are unable to relate. It was a Tuesday afternoon, and the husband had decided he no longer wanted to be married. He loved his wife, but her incessant behaviors surrounding the infertility had taken a toll on him.

How many times did he ask her to get help? How many times had they talked about seeing a therapist, but the focus was normally on conceiving? Every effort in the marriage went to trying to conceive and doing research. He had grown weary. Because there is a silent suffering associated and commonly attached to infertility, there was no outlet.

He could not talk to anyone because they decided not to share what was going on. For her to talk to someone would mean he was being exposed as well. How could they sustain a healthy marriage relationship if the level of toxicity was building month by month? Was she willing to listen to what he had to say? Was he willing to listen and consider everything she wanted to do on this journey?

Another significant challenge when faced with infertility is finances. It is important for spouses to communicate what their expectations will be and agree on a budget. Fertility treatments and associated doctors' visits are costly. When couples are already challenged financially, adding fertility treatments and medical bills can cause additional strain on the budget and the marriage.

That is a contributing factor to what happened with this couple. The two did not agree and they were not communicating well. The wife did not trust the husband would support her, so she often left him out. She left him out of decisions, considerations, conversations and stole the opportunity to have input from him.

Their marriage had the potential to thrive beyond the fertility issues. However, the wife's inability to trust her husband's leadership and consider his thoughts and feelings caused unnecessary discord. Their marriage was already experiencing periods of strain; however, the issues with fertility exacerbated them. Now, their marriage is hurting.

Marriage oneness is essential in every area of the marriage relationship and especially so when dealing with fertility issues. Your partner should be your truest confidante. Also, the relationship between husband and wife should be nurtured with or without a child. Keep that in mind as you navigate through this experience.

A Moment to H.O.P.E.

Have you experienced hurt in your marriage? Do you know what it feels like to block your spouse out intentionally or unintentionally? Have you made decisions regarding fertility and not included your spouse? Take a moment and consider times when your marriage was hurting. Take notes on your thoughts and reflect in the space provided. Once you have done so, take a moment and pray the prayer that follows.

Reflections

_____

_____

_____

_____

_____

_____

Prayer

Father, I have isolated myself in this marriage at times. Sometimes, I have left my husband out intentionally or unintentionally. I love my husband, but my desire to have a child has taken priority in my marriage. That does not align with your word or will for my life. God, help me to make better choices. Help me to include my husband, consider his feelings, hear his thoughts and give me peace. In Christ's name, I pray. Amen.

God's Word

For this reason a man shall leave his father and his mother, and shall be joined to his wife; and they shall become one flesh.
Genesis 2:24 (AMP)

You're NOT the Only One Suffering

As a woman, somehow, I thought that my inability to carry a child full-term and the "unexplained infertility" was something that affected only me. I was the one crying and pleading and praying. I was the one angry and frustrated with God. I was the one who felt like God hated me for choosing this for me.

I often found myself saying things like "I cannot believe this is happening to me" or "you don't care one way or another". For years, this was how I spoke. These words were my first response when conversing with my husband about circumstances, decisions and discussions related to conceiving.

I remember, as if it were yesterday, one conversation we had, specifically. We were discussing goals, plans and what waiting on God looks like. In true Sharhonda fashion, I made it about me. I referenced the miscarriage from Mother's Day 2008 and acted as if I alone experienced that tragedy. "You are NOT the only one who lost a child. I lost a child, also," he responded.

That was it! That was the first time I heard him speak as if he was a part of what was happening. Although it was the first time I HEARD HIM, it was not the first time he spoke about it. I was so consumed with making it my trial alone that I missed all the opportunities to pray for him. I missed the opportunities to comfort him and I left my man vulnerable. His voice that day and that statement changed how we walked this journey forever.

    I missed the opportunity to pray with and for my husband. I am reminded of God's word that tells us to be watchful (1 Peter 5:8[15]). I was so busy focusing on my own pain, fears, anger and shame, I didn't consider what my husband was feeling.

---

[15] 1 Peter 5:8 (ESV): Be sober-minded; be watchful. Your adversary the devil prowls around like a roaring lion, seeking someone to devour.

A Moment to H.O.P.E.

Have you considered this experience to be yours alone? Have you excluded your husband? Have you negated the fact that he also hurts, longs for a child or has lost a child in this process? Take a moment to think about how this has affected your marriage. As you reflect, write your thoughts in the space provided. If you have in any way been guilty of not inviting your spouse to grieve with you, pray the prayer that follows.

Reflections

_____

_____

_____

_____

_____

_____

Prayer

Father, forgive me for intentionally or unintentionally excluding my husband. Lord, I was selfish to believe that he was not affected or bothered by miscarriage or the trials and challenges of our "unexplained infertility" just as I was. Lord, help me to not be self-centered and to realize that we are in this together. Teach me how to meet my husband at his point of need on this journey and give us peace and strength. Help me to be watchful and to seek you in all things. In Christ's name. Amen.

God's Word

Be sober-minded; be watchful. Your adversary the devil prowls around like a roaring lion, seeking someone to devour. Resist him, firm in your faith, knowing that the same kinds of suffering are being experienced by your brotherhood throughout the world. And after you have suffered a little while, the God of all grace, who has called you to his eternal glory in Christ, will himself restore, confirm, strengthen, and establish you.
1 Peter 5:8-10 (ESV)

Do You Hear That?
Silent Suffering Speaks Volumes

I spent 11 years in silence. Those years were the hardest years of my life. I walked around with no one to talk to, angry that the feelings I had were trapped inside with nowhere to go. Honestly, I didn't feel that anyone would understand the pain I was experiencing.

  I had a few friends who walked with me through bouts of fertility challenges. One had a miscarriage. She and I would talk about our desires. When she ended up pregnant and then miscarried, we both cried. I cried for her as I knew her heart and she was someone I knew, knew my heart. Although she had children of her own, she was able to empathize with what I must have felt. That was important to me. It made me, in a sense, feel heard. My pain felt real and not just something I imagined.

  Today, while writing this, the first video I ever did where I mentioned infertility came up on my timeline memories. I shared it. It was 2017 and I FINALLY said something briefly in a Facebook Live message. The comment on infertility was hidden inside the message and I knew who listened to the full video by those who commented or reached out to me. Again, there were others who silently shared my pain, reaching out to me to commend me on being brave. Oh, but that was still just a whisper on this journey of silent suffering.

The next day, I cried. I didn't know why I was crying, and then it hit me. I WAS FREE! The secret I was carrying for over 11 years had been shared in a message I knew many would not hear. It did not matter who listened. It did not matter who heard it. The only thing that mattered is that I said IT. Saying IT Made Me Free!

A few months prior, I was speaking at a woman's tea referencing women in the Bible. When I spoke about Hannah, I began to choke up. My sister-in-love who was recording (and who had also held my secret) gave me THE LOOK! It was THE LOOK that held me together. We both knew, in that moment, I could not break down. What was important that day was that I began the healing process. I had made a comparison of me to Hannah to a room full of strangers (and a few close friends and family members). That was the catalyst to realizing the need to give voice to the silence. That was the day I knew my freedom was tied to my voice.

The inbox messages, text messages and calls I received about my quick mention of infertility sparked conversations and more and more women confirmed they, too, were suffering in silence. What a terrible thing that was! I was in bondage to my pain and finally there was hope. I was finding my voice and helping others find theirs. That is what I desire this book will do. I pray it will help others find their voice and end their personal silent suffering.

Throughout this journey and even through my silence, I knew that my testimony would lead to my freedom. Yet, even knowing that God's word says we are overcomers by the words of our testimonies (Revelations 12:11[16]), it did not give me the courage to speak up. I still hid behind the mask.

---

[16] Revelation 12:11 (ESV): And they have conquered him by the blood of the Lamb and by the word of their testimony, for they loved not their lives even unto death.

A Moment of H.O.P.E.

Have you suffered in silence because of your infertility challenges? Whether you have miscarried, tried to conceive, or are currently journeying through Barren Land, you may know what it feels like to suffer in silence. Take a moment as you reflect on this section and share your thoughts below. If you have been in bondage to suffering in silence, pray along the prayer that follows.

Reflections

_____

_____

_____

_____

_____

_____

_____

_____

Prayer

Father, I am tired. I am tired of being ashamed of dealing with infertility. I am tired of answering questions. I am tired of asking questions. I am tired of hiding my pain. I am tired of not having anyone to talk to. Lord, the blogs are not comforting and cause me to doubt, fear and suffer. Heavenly Father, I pray that you would give me the support I need for this journey. Give voice to my silence and end the suffering by giving me peace. In Christ's name, I pray. Amen.

God's Word

And let us not grow weary of doing good, for in due season we will reap, if we do not give up.

Galatians 6:9 (ESV)

Hello, My Name is Shame

Do you ever feel like the terrible things that have happened to you are your fault? As a Christian, it is challenging for me to walk in this. The shame associated with infertility is grievous, yet I have no control over my body. I am tired of walking around drenched in shame and saturated in grief.

When I talk to women about infertility, even those who do not know my story, I hear the stories of shame and the affects it has had on their lives. Why is it that we fail to realize the sovereignty of God in this area? I think one of the key themes here is control. We lack it and because there is nothing we can do – we are ashamed of our situation.

Certainly, we act as if we have the power to turn it around. Especially, when we hear that we should try other options, etc. Seriously, for women who have really walked the journey through Barren Land, they typically have exhausted all their options (at least those they were willing to consider). For my husband and I, we did not exhaust every option the doctor gave us. We did yield to the only option we knew. That option was and is to trust God and the plan He has for our lives.

Should we be ashamed for trusting God with our lives? Should we be ashamed about what God is doing in our lives? Well, this may be a little off topic; however, this is common whether people are reaping a harvest or experiencing a lack. Shame seems to be a common thread. When we are doing well and are flourishing, we feel like we don't want to talk about it for others may see it as boasting. In some instances, we are ashamed of how God has blessed us in comparison to others. Yet, when we are in a trial and we cannot see our way out, we are ashamed that God has "left us here".

What is the alternative to shame as it is associated with infertility? For me, it is surrender. Surrender to God's will for my life. Surrender to the realization and fact that I am not in control. Surrender to the peace that God is eager to give me if I just move out of my way.

God's word is paramount in how I overcome shame. I encourage you to wrap yourself in God's word and how He defines you. Consider shame in infertility as not being satisfied with how God has created you. Remember, there is NOTHING to be ashamed of because you do not have the power to conceive or change God's plan for your life. Surrender to His will and remember that, no matter what, you are wonderfully made, and no good thing will God withhold from you (Psalm 139:14[17], Psalm 84:11).

---

[17] Psalm 139:14 (ESV): I praise you, for I am fearfully and wonderfully made. Wonderful are your works; my soul knows it very well.

A Moment to H.O.P.E.

Have you experienced shame on your journey through Barren Land? Do any of these feelings ring familiar to you? If so, take a moment and share your thoughts below as you reflect on this discussion. When you are done, if you desire to, pray this prayer of hope on the following page.

Reflections

_____

_____

_____

_____

_____

_____

_____

_____

Prayer

Father, I know that you are sovereign, and my body belongs to you. Lord, help me to know that there is no shame in infertility whether it is explained or unexplained. The doctors described being unable to have a child, to term as "unexplained infertility". According to your word, I submit to you... accepting that infertility and the inability to bear children is a matter of will... your will. YOUR will is what I desire most of all, Lord. Help me to be free from shame and give me peace. In Christ's name, I pray. Amen.

God's Word

For the LORD God is a sun and shield; the LORD bestows favor and honor. No good thing does he withhold from those who walk uprightly.

Psalm 84:11 (ESV)

Everyone is Having a Baby Except Me

Once I moved to Charlotte, North Carolina, church was a place I was able to have peace even if I did not have it anywhere else. No one knew us there. There was no one asking THE QUESTIONS. No one constantly checking and touching my belly. There, no one knew us, our age, our marital status, or whether we had children and, actually, no one cared. That was different. It felt great.

How liberating was that? To be in a place where you didn't have to wonder what people were wondering (at least not about infertility). It was my safe place. As lonely as North Carolina was, FOR ME, it was a place where I could hide from EVERYONE who was waiting for me to have a child. I worked remotely; so, I was not typically faced with inquisitive coworkers. Because I traveled frequently to different places, I rarely saw the same people. So, the small talk about children and families was minimal. I escaped it without the constant pressure of explaining why I/WE didn't have children.

Then, a shift happened one Sunday. It was different. A heaviness came over me that I didn't recognize. Oh, but it was familiar. I experienced it before... but now, it had invaded my space.

My safe place was now exposed. I made it out of church that day. Although my husband noticed my countenance had changed as he typically does, he didn't acknowledge it; he just let me go through my emotions as he supported me and prayed for me. I got over it. That time.

A few more Sundays came and went before I stumbled on another. I was singing and that feeling came over me again. The choir was singing "It Is Well". I love that song. My Nana and I would sing it together. But this day... this day... I could not sing the song. I sank down in my seat. The person in front of me was pregnant. The person to the left of me was pregnant. As I walked out of the sanctuary, it seemed as if everyone was pregnant. Everyone except me. In that moment, it was NOT well.

That day, I decided I had a problem. It was bigger than I thought. I wanted to isolate myself. I didn't want to go outside. I didn't want to go to church. I didn't want to shop. I did not want to see ANOTHER PREGNANT WOMAN. It had become too much to bear. So, I cried. Then, I got help.

Whew, God's word and the hymns of the church surely have been my comfort on the journey through Barren Land chasing rainbows. If you know the hymns of the church and the promises of God's word, I encourage you to sing them, recite them, embrace them. They are a saving grace and a sweet refreshing in seasons of pain, grief, and uncertainty. One of my favorite comforting verses in those moments is Jeremiah 29:11[18]. God's plan for me did not include harm and I could surely rest in that.

---

[18] Jeremiah 29:11 (ESV): For I know the plans I have for you, declares the LORD, plans for welfare and not for evil, to give you a future and a hope.

A Moment of H.O.P.E.

Maybe you are familiar with feeling overwhelmed when you see pregnant women. Maybe you have friends who are/were pregnant, and you had to be happy. Maybe you, like me, have even had to host and plan baby showers for close friends and family. If so, you are not alone. As you reflect on this topic, take a moment and share your thoughts below. Once you have done so, pray the prayer of comfort that follows.

Reflections

_____

_____

_____

_____

_____

_____

_____

Prayer

Father, as your word says in Romans 12:15, we should rejoice with those who rejoice. Lord, help me to rejoice when others are blessed with the miracle of childbirth. Help me not to think more highly of myself than I ought by thinking that it should be me. Lord, give me the strength to be a source of encouragement to others. Remove the spirit of jealousy or envy if it is present and give me peace. In Christ Jesus' name, I pray. Amen.

God's Word

Rejoice with those who rejoice, weep with those who weep.
Romans 12:15 (ESV)

Why Do They Ask?

Have you talked about having children? Do you want to start a family right away? Have you discussed how many children you want? Are you open to adoption? What if he/she doesn't want children? Would you like a boy or a girl? Do either of you have children already? Oh, my goodness, yawl better get started! These questions/statements are some of the most common things people hear when they get married and, though absurd, as a Christian, it seems these questions/statements dominate most conversations.

It was early one afternoon, and I was standing with a few Christian women. My "sisters-in-Christ", if you will. One of the women among us had just had a miscarriage a few days earlier. Other women in the group were unaware. "I just miscarried" is not something you walk around broadcasting. I could empathize with the pain she was in. I knew of the grief she was experiencing, and I had not even experienced to that magnitude at that point.

What happened next shaped my future conversations forever. One of the women in the group turned to us (most of us were newly married) and said, "And when are YOU going to have some children (pointing to my friend)." My heart broke for my friend. This woman was asking each of us the same question, but when the question was aimed at my friend who recently miscarried, it felt different. The question hit a nerve. I wanted to protect her. I wanted to shield her from the questions people feel they have the freedom to ask. There was nothing I could do. I stood in silence and prayed. Prayed that my friend wouldn't break down in that moment. Prayed for the brokenness I knew my friend/sister-in-Christ was experiencing and prayed that I would NEVER ask a question that would jeopardize the peace of another. The only thought I had that day was, "Why do they ask?" Well, because they just do not know better. Maybe, I didn't either, until that day.

There is often no malicious intent (although I have experienced those who have had malicious intent) when people ask these questions. Most times, it is just common pleasantries, small talk, and chatter. However, it can trigger an unwelcomed emotion should the question be posed to someone who is struggling in this area. The innocence in these questions can provoke emotions that, in many cases, we wish would stay dormant.

I am grateful for the reminder of God's word in James 1[19] that says to be slow to speak, quick to hear, and slow to wrath. I learned from that scripture that silence is important at times. I pray you do not encounter these questions, however, if you do, I pray

---

[19] James 1:19 (ESV): Know this, my beloved brothers: let every person be quick to hear, slow to speak, slow to anger.

you will be slow to speak, trust the Lord for strength and know that God will carry you on the wings of compassion.

A Moment to H.O.P.E.

If you are familiar with the uncomfortable feeling of being asked questions about your future, your marriage, and your fertility, take a moment to reflect on this topic. As you think about it, share your thoughts below. If you feel lead, join in the prayer for comfort in times like these.

Reflections

_____

_____

_____

_____

_____

_____

Prayer

Lord, I know people ask questions with good intentions. Although it doesn't feel like it, I know that I cannot respond in anger. Lord, bridle my tongue. Shield me from those who seek to hurt me with their questions. Strengthen me when the conversations, questions and statements are overwhelming. Give me strength to trust you in this process and give me peace. In Christ's name, I pray. Amen.

God's Word

Count it all joy, my brothers, when you meet trials of various kinds, for you know that the testing of your faith produces steadfastness.
James 1:2-3 (ESV)

Choosing to Tell Your Story

Why is it that I was able to talk about everything except this? This was different. For years, I wrestled with being able to have this conversation, but this journey was not just about me. This journey was about my family. My husband and I were in this together. If one of us shared, both of us were exposed. So, timing and unity was important.

    I'm sure it is no secret that women have an easier time having conversations than men. However, in this case, because of our positions in the church, our story would not just be shared with women. If I shared it with one of my sisters-in-Christ, the likeliness was that they would share it with their husbands. If they shared it with their husbands, that made my husband vulnerable to the discussions if it came up. I didn't think that was my decision to make. Men deal differently and I understood that. So, I chose silence to protect us. However, I did so assuming silence is what he wanted.

    One evening, before a prayer fellowship, I was having a difficult time. It was one of the months I believed I had miscarried. I had gotten to the point that I didn't have to go to the doctor for them to tell me what I already knew. After a few times miscarrying, I would stop going to the doctor. By the time I would get there, the

HCG levels would be so low they couldn't tell me anything but what I already knew. I was no longer pregnant. At the prayer fellowship, during prayer I broke down. I shared with the ladies in that room that I had miscarried. I almost couldn't breathe. I was so angry with God. I was praying. I was serving. I was trusting. I was longing to give birth to a child, and I was barren. I was bruised. I was broken.

I didn't know it at the time but choosing to tell those women made a difference. In that moment, I was not a prisoner to my circumstance. I was not alone. I was not suffering in silence. It ended there. My temporary freedom ended that night. I didn't talk about it much after that. I didn't want to have those hard conversations. Shame had paralyzed me and ushered me into my silent suffering. I settled into a place of isolation, anger, and fear.

As years went by, I would tell my story to people I didn't know. This was normally through casual conversations with strangers who may have mentioned it. People I thought would not judge me. Maybe, by year 10, I was beginning to realize the only way to be free was to give voice to the silence. And so, it began. I began to share. I shared with strangers. People in other countries who would never see me again heard bits of my story. At home, though, fear, shame, and embarrassment kept me hostage to my suffering and my silence roared on the inside.

"Is something wrong?" "You can talk to me if you ever need a shoulder to cry on?" "I understand and I know how you feel?" are just a few things that people would say. I would hear them, but I never believed it. This secret. This suffering. This was mine. This story was mine. The silence spoke volumes, but until now, it had to be that way. I had to hide to shield me from judgement and being labeled defective by others.

My wish is that I had chosen to speak sooner. I wish the women in my family had spoken up. I wish others who suffered in silence would have given it a voice. Since they didn't – I will!

Although this journey has been the most challenging experience I have faced, it has built levels of character in me I couldn't imagine I needed or would exist. I am a Christian before anything else. God's word has been my sustaining grace. God's plan for my life has carried me through every valley experience and it can do the same for you. God is sovereign. He does ALL things well. He is a rewarder of those that diligently seek Him and because of God's grace, I survived. God kept me through the most challenging times; I could NOT imagine this journey without the protection, promise and plan of the Lord my God.

I pray you can find strength in God's plan and promise for your life.

A Moment to H.O.P.E.

Have you been suffering in silence? Have you chosen to keep your story a secret? Do you have a story to tell? Are you comfortable with your silence? If you can relate to this topic take a moment and think about YOUR story. As you reflect, write your thoughts and prayers below. When you are finished, if lead, pray the prayer of comfort that follows.

Reflections

_____

_____

_____

_____

_____

_____

_____

Prayer

Father, I hurt for the women who have a story to tell yet suffer in silence. Women like me, who feel they are alone, who hurt, and whose voice is silenced by shame, fear, guilt, and embarrassment. Lord, according to your plan for my life, give voice to the silence these women and couples face. Give them the strength to stand on your will and plan and to walk boldly knowing you are good. Write my story Father, and give me the peace, passion, and power to share it. In Christ Jesus' name, I pray. Amen.

God's Word

Seek the Lord and his strength; seek his presence continually!
1 Chronicles 16:11 (ESV)

God Has NOT Failed You

Being angry with God was not difficult. All I did was reflect on His word and I would shatter from the inside out.

- "Behold, children are a heritage from the LORD, the fruit of the womb a reward" Psalm 127:3.
- "Be fruitful and multiply…" Genesis 1:28.
- "And Isaac prayed to the LORD for his wife, because she was barren. And the LORD granted his prayer, and Rebekah his wife conceived" Genesis 25:21.
- "He gives the barren woman a home, making her the joyous mother of children. Praise the LORD!" Psalm 113:9.

I'm sure you get my point here. I would read these scriptures, hope, and pray. Why were these scriptures in the Bible if they weren't going to apply to me? Aren't I supposed to believe in the entire Bible? Isn't every word of God true? If so, then why weren't these scriptures true for me? Why was there no fruit of my womb? Why did Kirey's prayers go unanswered? Why wasn't I the joyous mother of children?

God are you even real? Are you listening? Are you there? How is it that you have called me to do a thing that you will NOT allow me to do? You have the power to do it, but you don't. Where are you God and why are you NOT answering my prayers? God, are you kidding me? This must be a joke.

I laugh at myself now. I mean... really? Here is where I am reminded that God says, "Be angry and do not sin" (Ephesians 4:26 ESV). There were days when I just wanted to give up. I was tired. I was hopeless. What was my purpose? Why was I living? If I was not going to have children... if God was not going to answer me, then what was it all for? Why was I here? God, for sure, in my mind, had failed me. For that, I had no reason to live. Those were hard days.

It's amusing to me as I think of it now. Really, Sharhonda? You have no reason to live because God did not allow you to have children? How ridiculous was that? Very! I had resigned myself to the untruth (the absolute lie) that God didn't love me as I thought He did. My new thing was, "I am good enough to care for, yet not good enough to bare."

Because God always allowed me to help raise and nurture other children, it made me bitter and resentful. Now, I know that the God I love and serve, the God that had/has a plan for me for a future and to do me no harm (Jeremiah 29:11 ESV) is working all things out for my good (Romans 8:28[20]). My God, Jesus, the lover of

---

[20] Romans 8:28 (ESV): And we know that for those who love God all things work together for good, for those who are called according to his purpose.

my soul, has not failed me. In the sovereignty of God, He knew and knows best, and His will is what I want.

As I reflect on this season of my life and those times when I fought to trust God's word, I pray for you. I pray for you as you read these pages, as you reflect on your personal journey and as you seek God's face for your strength, peace and direction. I pray for you as you have moments of doubt and I ask the Lord to allow you to move past the maladaptive thoughts that hold you hostage. It is not my will that any of you experience the pain and anguish that accompanies lies and schemes the enemy tells us to keep us from trusting God. I pray you would find peace in God's perfect will for your life and for your family.

A Moment to H.O.P.E.

Has your journey in Barren Land caused you to feel unwanted, less than and like God has failed you? Have you mulled over and combed through the scriptures and found stories or verses that shape how you feel about God and His plan for your life? If this topic is familiar to you, take a few moments to reflect on some of the scriptures mentioned above. Take note on how they affect you and share your thoughts in the space provided. If you're so inclined, whisper these words of prayer that follows to comfort and give you peace.

Reflections

_____

_____

_____

_____

_____

_____

Prayer

Father, I know you are sovereign. Forgive me for being selfish and in my flesh. God, I know you care for me. I know you love me, and you have the perfect plan for my life. Lord, continue to carry me on this journey with peace and strength as you lead me through Barren Land! In Jesus' name, I pray. Amen.

God's Word

For I know the plans I have for you, declares the LORD, plans for welfare and not for evil, to give you a future and a hope.
Jeremiah 29:11 (ESV)

Finding Purpose in Pain

These tears are different. Over the past few weeks, I realized that after 13 years, I FINALLY HAD PEACE! I did not recognize it. I almost didn't remember what it felt like. It felt new. I had been walking in grief, fear, shame, sadness, sorrow, jealousy, embarrassment, envy, despair, anxiety, anticipation, depression, and discontent for over a decade. Some or all these emotions, were felt at some point over the decade on this journey. Some more than others *and* I had even experienced them all, overwhelmingly, at the same time.

    I knew pain so well, but I had learned to hide it even better. I had mastered the mask that I lived beneath and had learned that I did not have to share my sorrow. Honestly, who was welcoming it? Who was welcoming me? I mentioned it earlier, but I remember almost sharing my testimony at a women's tea. I knew it wasn't the time or the place for that unveiling. Not because they wouldn't show love but it's important to stay on task and be respectful to the leading of the Lord. Thank God for my sister-in-love who from behind the camera gave me that "YOU BETTER NOT" look and my sister-in-Christ who was sitting even closer that finished the look off for her! I wasn't ready. I was still in pain. I was still angry. I was still hurting, and I had not fully realized my purpose in this journey.

Today, I know. After I received a few comments and messages from my Facebook Live video where I briefly mentioned my struggle with infertility, I knew I had purpose through this journey. Giving voice to those suffering and turning up the volume on the silence. I will not let the next generation of girls in my family wait too long. I will not act as if there is nothing wrong. I know the doctors said its "unexplained infertility" and I understand this is God's will for my life; however, for those who want to explore other options, I want to give them all the information I have.

Today, I want to ensure women around the world know they are not alone. If no one else is with them, I am standing with women everywhere to tell them it's ok. For Christians who feel that God's promises are being withheld, I stand with them and remind them of the sovereignty of God. For women who feel their husbands are not affected by this journey, I stand with them to teach them how to encourage their husbands as they encourage themselves.

Journeying through Barren Land and chasing rainbows taught me a lot. And I am still learning. This is and was the road to my purpose. Women everywhere need to hear from me. This book is just a glimpse into what this journey has been for me. God has equipped me with the key to unlock the chains that keep other women bound. I am here for it. I am ready. I am available. Singing to myself, "If you can use anyone Lord, you can use me."

What a powerful testimony to know God chose me for this. He trusted you and me with this thorn in our flesh. He is strengthening me for this journey, and I am ready.

I am praying for you couples who are on the brink of a breakthrough. I am praying for you couples who have exhausted your options. I am praying for you couples who have experienced your rainbow baby and I am praying for you couples who may never experience the miracle of childbirth.

I AM PRAYING.

"Infertility is not a death sentence. Infertility is not punishment. Infertility is nothing to be ashamed of. Infertility is not created to ruin your marriage. God was, God is, and God always will be fully in control of our lives. In this, I have purpose".

~ *Sharhonda L. Ford*

A Moment to H.O.P.E.

Has purpose been something you struggled to find and pain something you struggle to rid yourself of on this journey through Barren Land? Are you familiar with the pain and lack of purpose associated with journeying through Barren Land? If anything in this section spoke to your heart, take a moment to think about it. As you reflect, share your thoughts on how you can find purpose in pain in the midst of your trial in the space provided. Once you have done so, feel free to pray this prayer of comfort.

Reflections

_____

_____

_____

_____

_____

_____

Prayer

Father, I love you. Thank you for turning my scars into stars and giving me purpose through this pain. Lord, it is no secret that I never would have made it without you. Forgive me for doubting you had a purpose for me beneath this sorrow and pain. Lord, I am so grateful that you chose me. As I continue this journey, saturate me with your peace and fill me with unspeakable joy as I give voice to the silence and share the key that unlocks the chains of the bondage of infertility. I love you, Father God. In Jesus' name. Amen.

God's Word

Therefore, confess your sins to one another and pray for one another, that you may be healed. The prayer of a righteous person has great power as it is working.

James 5:16 (ESV)

Triumph from Tragedy
(Accepting what God Allows)

As I crossed the street, I smiled and felt a feeling of great accomplishment. I had just spent the afternoon shopping. In church, I sat with mothers, watched Kirey hold babies and witnessed the numerous soon-to-be parents in our small group and around the church. I wasn't bothered. I wasn't hurt. I wasn't sad. I was glad. Glad to know that others were experiencing the gift of life through pregnancy and childbirth. I found joy in knowing there were women who were not (in that season) experiencing the pain, sorrows, and grief of infertility. I knew this didn't mean they weren't familiar with it. I knew it didn't mean they wouldn't experience it. It just meant, in that moment, they were free from that pain.

Pom-Pom's waving in the air, music playing loudly, and people rejoicing. That is what it feels like in this season of my life. Wait! Don't get too excited. It has only been a few months. However, I am so excited for this change. I am excited for this peace. I am excited for this season as I experience joy in the journey.

I am at a pivotal point in this journey. Barren Land is a place I will always be connected to; however, it is not a place that I will allow to continue to define me. It will not define who I am. Barren Land will not define who I will become. It is a part of me. It is a part of my journey. It is NOW the place that fuels me. It is the catalyst that gives other women hope through Christ in me.

Many days, I thought my life was over with no reason to live. I was ashamed that I couldn't naturally give my husband what we both desired. I was bitter that this was my lot in life. I was angry that God saw fit to NOT let this cup pass from me and I felt defeated. The tragedies of miscarriages, failed attempts with assisted fertility and the knowledge that we would never hold the babies we created or carried overwhelmed me.

Today, I am no longer a prisoner to that pain. Today, I am FREE. Yes, I am Fearless – Restored – Empowered – Eager to take my tragedy and live triumphantly in the hope I have in Christ. The hope that *"Being confident of this very thing, that he which hath begun a good work in you will perform it until the day of Jesus Christ."* (Philippians 1:6 KJV). *That* is VICTORY.

A Moment of H.O.P.E.

Have you been able to find triumph in the perceived tragedy of infertility? Are you still seeking the victory as you journey through Barren Land? As you reflect on the topic above, take a moment and share your thoughts below. When you are done, join in this prayer for victory in Jesus.

Reflections

_____

_____

_____

_____

_____

_____

_____

Prayer

Heavenly Father, this journey has been difficult. We have laughed and cried over these pages. Miscarriage and infertility are painful. The emotions associated with it are debilitating and paralyzing, but we know there is victory in Jesus. Lord, we need you. We need your love. We need your joy. We need your peace. Strengthen us for this journey and show us the victory. In Christ Jesus' name, we pray. Amen.

God's Word

Being confident of this very thing, that he which hath begun a good work in you will perform it until the day of Jesus Christ.

Philippians 1:6 (KJV)

Too Soon to Tell

> "Stillbirth is when a baby dies in the womb after 20 weeks of pregnancy. Most stillbirths happen before a woman goes into labor, but a small number happen during labor and birth. Stillbirth affects about 1 in 100 pregnancies each year in the United States; this is about 1 percent of all pregnancies and about 24,000 babies."
>
> www.marchofdimes.org/complications/stillbirth.aspx
>
> "Miscarriage (also called early pregnancy loss) is when a baby dies in the womb (uterus) before 20 weeks of pregnancy. For women who know they're pregnant, about 10 to 15 in 100 pregnancies (10 to 15 percent) end in miscarriage. Most miscarriages happen in the first trimester before the 12th week of pregnancy. Miscarriage in the second trimester (between 13 and 19 weeks) happens in 1 to 5 in 100 (1 to 5 percent) pregnancies."
>
> www.marchofdimes.org/complications/miscarriage.aspx

One woman expressed the terrible grief that was associated with her miscarriage. One of the greatest mysteries to me surrounding pregnancy announcements is why we have/need to wait until we are three months before we can share it. I understand the rationale, I just do not understand the reason. The most common reason I hear is that you don't want to tell anyone in case you lose the baby. Wouldn't that position me to have to cope with the loss privately if I do not get to share it with anyone?

"It's too soon to tell." If life begins at conception, shouldn't we be able to talk about life at conception? "You don't want to celebrate too soon". Shouldn't we celebrate the gift of life even if we do not carry the baby to term? Now, don't get me wrong. I do understand how difficult it is to grieve a miscarriage; however, doesn't that same difficulty exist whether you tell someone or not?

For a moment, let me just talk aloud about this. Imagine having your 1st positive pregnancy test. The excitement cannot be contained! You want to tell someone, but you can't because you've learned or have been warned NOT to share the news too soon. Imagine that happening repeatedly for years and each time you do not share it for fear you will miscarry again. You've ended up never sharing the joy of your pregnancy (which it is a joy from the very beginning) and never having anyone to share in the sorrow of your loss. That's a lonely experience. Which leads me to wonder, "What *do* you get to share?"

I have an idea! How about we learn how to encourage others who are experiencing loss? What if we stop telling people not to feel? What if we stop saying "you gotta be strong" or "it will be ok"? What if we stand in the gap with and for someone? I believe I would rather have someone share in my loss than walk around in silence and suffer alone. How about you?

A Moment of H.O.P.E.

Have you experienced this silent suffering in anger? Sometimes, it is difficult to know what the best action is based on fear, feelings (which sometimes lie), and the societal standard. For me, I learned silent suffering IS the loudest cry ever! Take a moment and share your thoughts in the space provided below. Once you have done so, join me in prayer for peace, guidance and forgiveness.

Reflections

_____

_____

_____

_____

_____

_____

_____

Prayer

Father, we know that you are sovereign, with and for us. God we also know that in anger we may fail to acknowledge your sovereignty and rejoice in your will and plan for our lives. BUT, today, we ask you to forgive us for our anger toward you and our lack of faith in your plan for us; for we know that your plan is best for us. We trust your plan for our lives. Temper my emotions when the enemy attempts to persuade us that we are damaged and unloved by you. I love you, Father. In Jesus' name. Amen.

God's Word

Blessed be the God and Father of our Lord Jesus Christ, the Father of mercies and God of all comfort, who comforts us in all our affliction, so that we may be able to comfort those who are in any affliction, with the comfort with which we ourselves are comforted by God.
2 Corinthians 1:3-4 (ESV)

Saturated in Shame

I had a follow-up appointment at the fertility center. Oddly, I always felt a sense of fear and shame at the thought of running into someone I knew. Yes, I know now how silly that was. If anyone I knew was there, then it was likely they were there for the same reason I was!

I walked in to register and to sign in for my appointment. In my peripheral vision, I saw someone from church. My immediate response was to be startled and shame filled my heart. What if she tells someone I was here? Did she see me? Does she recognize me?

I laugh now as I remember this. It must be one of the most ridiculous of the MANY ridiculous things that happened on this journey. Our eyes locked and we did a slight nod of the head in acknowledgement of one another. We each continued with what we were doing and never spoke of it.

For months and maybe years, I wondered what she thought about me being there. I wondered why *we* could not have a conversation about it. Why was it that I saw a sister-in-Christ in a place where many women dread being and I could not even embrace her, comfort her, encourage her or at most share in her sorrow.

We were sometimes in meetings together. Served at different events and sat on the same ministries. We sat across from each other and even stood gathered with women together and nothing was ever said. There was no mention of us meeting there. A few years later, the Lord blessed her with the opportunity to grow her family. I was happy for her and wondered, did it work? What was different for her? All the questions I had for her went unanswered because the shame was too paralyzing to approach her.

God's word really lights my pathways (Psalm 119:105[21]). Thankfully, as I reflect on the saturation of shame in my heart at times, I focused on Isaiah 50:7[22] which says that I should not be ashamed. Shame debilitates. Along my journey, my life was filled with shame (suffering, hiding, anger, misery, envy). But today I am free. Free from suffering. Free from hiding. Free from anger. Free from misery. Free from envy. Free from SHAME. I am walking in boldness and purpose. The struggle is part of my story. The chains of shame are broken, and the victory of healing is mine. I no longer walk in fear and embarrassment. My mind is saturated with God's

---

[21] Psalm 119:105 (ESV): Your word is a lamp to my feet and a light to my path.
[22] Isaiah 50:7 (ESV): But the Lord God helps me; therefore I have not been disgraced; therefore I have set my face like a flint, and I know that I shall not be put to shame.

peace. My heart is saturated with God's love. My spirit is saturated with God's joy. The same is available to you. Be free today!

A Moment of H.O.P.E.

If you have encountered shame and fear of someone seeing you at a fertility location or doctor's appointment, take a few minutes and write down what you feel as you reflect on that time. Once you have done so, think about what you would do differently and how you can replace the feelings of shame and embarrassment with peace and hope for God's plan for your life. If you are inclined, pray aloud or within the prayer of comfort that follows.

Reflections

_____

_____

_____

_____

_____

_____

Prayer

Father, I understand that shame has saturated my heart and mind at times on this journey. It is difficult to think differently and to accept your will and plan. Lord, sometimes, I fear the judgement and opinions of others. I desire, Lord, to block fear and embrace faith. Remind me to walk in boldness and reject shame and embarrassment. Help me to use my walk through Barren Land as a testimony and encouragement to others. Help me NOT to feel defective or less than. In Jesus' name, I pray. Amen.

God's Word

For the Lord GOD will help me; therefore, shall I not be confounded: therefore, have I set my face like a flint, and I know that I shall not be ashamed.

Isaiah 50:7 (ESV)

Forgiveness – Abortion and Infertility

Often when I speak to women who have experienced abortion (be it elective or medically recommended) there is a great bit of guilt associated with that decision. As Christians, it is important to remember that God's grace IS enough.

I have heard people blame failures, disappointments, trials, tragedies, misfortunes and other life happenings and events to sin and poor decisions made. One of the common threads with women on the infertility journey who have had an elective abortion is, "The infertility is due to the abortion." Imagine the guilt and shame associated with this level of thinking. Yes, I feel confident and know there are consequences for our sin; however, I do not believe we have the power to dictate and determine what our consequence will be.

Women have struggled with the decision of abortion and childbirth since the beginning of time. For some, the decision may have been reckless, without consideration, or fear (just to name a few). For others, the decision may have been due to medical recommendation, rape, or other reasons seemingly justifiable. Whatever the reason for abortion, determining your infertility is based on that decision yields shame, guilt, depression and other powerful emotions with the ability to paralyze and render you powerless.

God's forgiveness is available for everyone. It does not matter what the sin is, God's forgiveness reaches to you. I urge women who struggle with this flawed thinking to pray for God's forgiveness in that area and release yourself from the guilt, shame and pain of that decision. Remember, you do NOT have the power to dictate or determine what God will do as a result of your sin. God's grace and mercy extends to every one of us. Don't forfeit your peace by refusing to pray. Don't hold yourself hostage to the decisions of your past. Repent. Release. Revive. God is for you and His plan is greater than any decision you have made. Believe that and move forward by faith.

A Moment of H.O.P.E.

If you are familiar with the shame and judgement of abortion, whether public or private, today is the day to be free. As a point of reference, there are other things women blame infertility on, such as drinking, smoking, or pre-marital sex. No matter what sins you have committed, God's will and plan for your life will ALWAYS override it. You do NOT have the power to alter God's sovereign plan. Take a moment and reflect on your feelings surrounding your decisions and repent. Use the space provided to share your thoughts as a point of reflection. Once you have done so, pray the prayer that follows.

Reflections

_____

_____

_____

_____

_____

Prayer

Father, I thank you for your word and the forgiveness available to me. You are such a good, good Father and I thank you. Lord, I have been distracted by the guilt of decisions made in the past. I focus too often on my sin and not on you as my Savior. From this day forward, I release my fears, shame, doubt, guilt and everything associated with those sinful decisions to you. Thank you for the freedom provided through your forgiveness and the peace with your presence. I walk boldly in it as I trust your plan on my journey through Barren Land. Lord, I thank you. In Jesus' name, I pray. Amen.

God's Word

He will again have compassion on us; he will tread our iniquities underfoot. You will cast all our sins into the depths of the sea.
Micah 7:19 (ESV)

A Chat with the Author

What is God's plan for you and your husband? — This may not be the end of the journey for you AND your journey MAY end in childbirth. However, the most important thing is to go through this journey with God. Whether, you are in the beginning stages, have been here for some time, or are exhausted by the journey through Barren Land Chasing Rainbows, I encourage you to take the love of Jesus with you.

God's love crosses every bridge, reaches every mountain, shields us through every fire, comforts us in every storm and prevents us from being consumed by the raging waters of life, including the journey of infertility chasing rainbows. I must admit, I spent so many years of this journey alone. I did not trust God's plan. For years, I was too broken to pray (depending on the season) and at the end of the day, I struggled to believe God would do it. Transparency is easy for me now. I only wish I had chosen this path at the beginning of my journey through Barren Land as I chased rainbows.

Maybe God's will *is* that you do not give birth to a child. It is NOT the end of the world (although, at times, it may feel like it). Learning to deal with the forever reminders that you did not bare children is pivotal to your journey. Understanding that you have value regardless is priceless and will strengthen you for the rest of your life.

Here are a few things that may help on this journey:

- Choose grace for yourself
- Choose grace for your spouse
- Choose forgiveness
- Choose faith
- Choose to believe God's will IS what you want.

TODAY, I am free. I am no longer a prisoner to the pain, fear, shame, once had me bound. This is my prayer for you. I want YOU to be free. I want freedom to be yours TODAY. Afterall, it IS available. Choose freedom. Choose forgiveness. Choose faith. Chasing Rainbows is about trusting God's plan, embracing God's promise, and yielding to the sovereign will of God for your life.

Biography

Psychotherapist, Sharhonda Ford is the Owner of Sharhonda L. Ford, Counseling, Coaching and Consulting. She is a licensed clinical mental health counselor (LCMHC) and a nationally certified counselor (NCC). She is in private practice and focuses on trauma with women and girls as well as couples work.

With a strong faith in the Lord Jesus Christ, Sharhonda is committed to excellence and shares a powerful testimony of overcoming tragedy, rebounding from loss, triumphing in trials, living beyond collision, and moving beyond the mask (her ministry of reconciliation).

Sharhonda has been married for 14 years to her best friend and life partner, Deacon Kirey Ford. She is a devoted wife, daughter, sister, and friend. She and her husband facilitate marriage counseling and group discussions on marriage, waiting, courtship and preparing for marriage.

Sharhonda stands firm on the unadulterated word of God and exclaims that she is not ashamed of the Gospel of Jesus Christ. Sharhonda's life verses are Philippians 4:6-9 and Psalm 84:11. Sharhonda's goal is to dispense H.O.P.E – Help Overcoming Powerful Emotions – to every client and person she meets.

For Speaking Engagement Inquiries email:

SharhondaFordSpeaks@gmail.com

Resources

OSHUN Fertility	https://www.oshunfertility.com
The Broken Brown Egg	http://thebrokenbrownegg.org
The Cade Foundation	https://www.cadefoundation.org
Fertility for Colored Girls	https://www.fertilityforcoloredgirls.org
The National Infertility Association	https://resolve.org

Because Infertility may cause significant Mental Health concerns it is important for me, as a clinician, to include the National Suicide Prevention Information

https://suicidepreventionlifeline.org

1-800-273-8255

Podcast: That Infertility CHIC

IG: @that_infertility_chic

Facebook: @thatinfertilitychic

Twitter: @infertilitychic

Email: Sharhondafordspeaks@gmail.com

www.ingramcontent.com/pod-product-compliance
Lightning Source LLC
Chambersburg PA
CBHW071445070526
44578CB00001B/219